主审 万正方

实用英语基础口译教程

A PRACTICAL COURSE OF BASIC ENGLISH INTERPRETATION

（修订本）

主　编　彭典贵
副主编　杜　敏
编　者　田林未　杜　敏　汪　莹
　　　　单　谊　倪世芳　彭典贵

U0361855

清华大学出版社
北京交通大学出版社
·北京·

内 容 简 介

本教材共分为 18 个单元和附录部分，是专门为具有基本的英语知识和应用能力的学习者编写的一部语言和技巧并重的基础阶段口译教材。目的在于使学习者通过本教材的学习，将所学的英语知识和能力"盘活"和"变现"。本教材的特色是实用性、基础性、时效性。

本教材适用于高等院校英语专业学生的初级口译课教学和基础阶段口译考试，也可供从事口译、外事、外贸、旅游等的涉外人员使用。

图书在版编目（CIP）数据

实用英语基础口译教程／彭典贵主编. — 修订本. — 北京：清华大学出版社；北京交通大学出版社，2010. 11（2023. 2 重印）

ISBN 978 - 7 -81123 -772 -6

Ⅰ. ①实… Ⅱ. ①彭… Ⅲ. ①英语 - 口译 - 高等学校 - 教材 Ⅳ. ①H315. 9

中国版本图书馆 CIP 数据核字（2010）第 079222 号

责任编辑：张利军
出版发行：清 华 大 学 出 版 社　　邮编：100084　　电话：010 - 62776969　　http：//www. tup. com. cn
　　　　　北京交通大学出版社　　邮编：100044　　电话：010 - 51686414　　http：//press. bjtu. edu. cn
印 刷 者：北京鑫海金澳胶印有限公司
经　　销：全国新华书店
开　　本：185 mm ×260 mm　　印张：12. 5　　字数：312 千字
版 印 次：2020 年 4 月第 1 版第 1 次修订　　2023 年 2 月第 8 次印刷
定　　价：36. 00 元

Preface

面向 21 世纪的中国比历史上任何时期更需要大量的口译人才来构筑和加固对外交往的桥梁。北京奥运会的成功举办和中国上海世博会的举办,使全国范围内的外语热悄然升温,为国家培养大批合格的口译人才已成为当务之急。在此大背景下,一部时效性、针对性、实用性强的口译教材对于培养高素质的口译人才是至关重要的。本教材正是为适应这一新的发展形势和需要而编写的。

《实用英语基础口译教程》是专门为具有基本的英语知识和应用能力的学生编写的一部语言和技巧并重的基础阶段口译教材,目的在于使学生通过本教材的学习,在较短时间内熟悉各种交际场合使用的英语语体,掌握基本的口译要领,培养准确实用的口译能力,从而使学生将所学的英语知识和能力"盘活"和"变现"。

1. 教材的特色

本教材具有以下特色。

(1)实用性。本教材依据口译的职业要求、工作特点、题材范围、教学效果而取材编写,教材内容密切联系当前国际、国内的实际情况,选材广泛实用,学生学后即可用于实践。本教材可帮助学习者通过相关的英语口译基础能力考试,实现学习内容与就业岗位的"零距离"。

(2)基础性。通过大量的口译实践,初步掌握影子跟读、速记、复述、数字口译、顺译、视译等基础阶段的技巧。本教材要求学习者在模仿、听辨原语语音的同时能借助主题和认知知识进行分析、综合、推理,达到正确理解所听到的信息,然后利用笔记或者短时记忆理解语篇意义,在讲话人完成一段讲话后迅速、准确、完整地用目的语表达原语信息的目的。

(3)时效性。为解决口译教材易老化和非口语化等常见问题,所选材料篇幅众多,注重题材的广泛性和内容的时效性,均为近些年来政治生活、社会生活、经济活动和教育事业等方面的热点话题和与时代同步的语言信息。

2. 教材的结构

本教材共分为 18 个单元和附录部分。其中,第 1 单元为口译基础知识和基础阶段口译技巧的概述,其余各单元按待人接物、校园生活、观光旅游、购物美食、时尚运动、休闲娱乐、节日习俗、求职招聘、商务礼仪、企业形象、经济发展、环境保护、科学技术、网络时代、文化差异、天灾人祸、社会问题等 17 个不同的主题展开。

每个单元由以下几部分组成。

Ⅰ.学习目标

Ⅱ.单元词汇

Ⅲ. 词组口译 $\begin{cases} \text{A. 英译汉} \\ \text{B. 汉译英} \end{cases}$

Ⅳ. 单句口译 $\begin{cases} \text{A. 英译汉} \\ \text{B. 汉译英} \end{cases}$

Ⅴ. 对话口译

Ⅵ. 短文口译 $\begin{cases} \text{A. 英译汉} \\ \text{B. 汉译英} \end{cases}$

Ⅶ. 强化训练 $\begin{cases} \text{1. 英语影子练习} \\ \text{2. 记忆、笔记练习} \\ \text{3. 数字听译练习} \\ \text{4. 习语口译练习} \\ \text{5. 句子顺译练习} \\ \text{6. 段落视译练习} \end{cases}$

3. 教材的使用

本教材可供 1 学年使用，每单元的教学学时为 4 学时。在具体使用过程中，教师可根据教学实际对单元内容进行取舍。为了方便课堂教学和学生自主学习，本教材配有供教学使用的 MP3 和练习参考答案，读者可先扫描封底上的防盗二维码，获取权限后，再扫描教材中每单元开始处的资源二维码获取电子资源。

本教材由彭典贵担任主编，杜敏担任副主编。各位编者的编写分工如下：彭典贵负责编写第 1 ~ 7 单元及附录部分；汪莹负责编写第 8、9 单元；田林未、倪世芳负责编写第 10 ~ 12 单元；单谊负责编写第 13 ~ 15 单元；杜敏负责编写第 16 ~ 18 单元。此外，彭典贵还负责全书的内容构思、体例安排、统稿和部分单元图片的选取。

在本教材出版之际，首先衷心感谢北京交通大学出版社张利军同志对本教材的出版做出的不懈努力。此外，还要特别感谢同济大学外国语学院万正方教授在百忙之中对书稿进行了认真的审校，并提出了宝贵的修改意见。

本教材适用于高等院校英语专业学生的初级口译课程教学和基础阶段口译考试，也可供从事口译、外事、外贸、旅游等行业的涉外人员使用。

在本教材编写过程中，我们参考并借鉴了国内外出版的有关书籍和相关的网站资料，在此谨表谢意！

由于口译工作具有很强的实践性和操作性，本教材在编写过程中力求题材广泛、情景真实、语言经典、表达规范、操作容易。尽管各位编者多次就稿件进行自校和互校，遗漏错讹仍在所难免，衷心希望同行专家及读者在使用过程中惠予指正。

编　者

2020 年 4 月

Contents

Unit 1

Introduction
口译概说

一、口译及其特点

（一）口译

众所周知，口译是当今社会一个炙手可热的职业，许多人试图通过多种途径的努力拿到这个"金饭碗"。但是，口译"这口饭"却不是太好吃的，因为除了个人的天资，还要求口译员必须具备"领悟力强""反应敏捷""记忆力好""口齿伶俐"等条件；在思想修养方面，要求口译员热爱祖国，责任心强，必须具有高尚的职业道德；在语言素质方面，要求口译员下苦功，做到听、说、读、写、译全面发展。

口译是人类在相互交往中通过两种语言的转换，准确、快速地传递信息，交流思想，讨论问题或解决问题的一种口头交际活动，是人类在跨文化、跨民族的交往活动中所依赖的一种基本交际手段。口译并不是对单词进行口头翻译，它是用目的语为别人准确地揭示和说明原语的意思。口译就是交流，即对原语进行分析，并把它译成听者能听懂的形式。因此，口译员不是研究语言某一特定方面的语言学家，而是对其工作实践中使用的语言掌握了丰富的、直观的知识的从业人员。

（二）口译的特点

口译与笔译可以说是翻译的两个方面，有相同的目标、相同的原则。虽然这两个词常常用"翻译"一词概括，但两者实际上却有不少的差异。

口译是一种特殊的语言交际过程，速度快是其首要特点。口译的全过程，从语言信息的接收、解码、记忆、编码到输出只在短短的瞬间进行。口译员一旦进入工作状态就像一台运转的机器，必须全神贯注、连续不断地进行语言信息的处理和转换工作。而且，口译的效果往往是立竿见影、当场见效。即使口译员对口译的效果不够满意，也难以返工或更改。

口译是一项艰苦而紧张的脑力劳动。口译员要面对各种意想不到的挑战，承受很大的思想压力。首先是无法完全预测交际双方的谈话内容，因而无从事先做充分的准备。其次，口译过程中口译员随时可能遇到语言、知识、文化等诸多方面的困难和障碍。另外，口译员可能在各种气氛紧张的现场进行口译，因此口译员工作时必须精力充沛，思想高度集中，做到耳、眼、手、脑、口并用，力求既迅速高效，又准确无误，既忠于原意，又灵活变通。所以，口译是一项极富挑战性的工作。

口译作为信息交流和交际传播的一部分，其信息覆盖很难有一个限定的边界。从其特点来看，其内容包罗万象，上至天文、下至地理，无所不包。因此，口译员须有扎实的语言功底、良好的心理素质、娴熟的语符转换技能，更须有一定的口才和良好的口译技能。

二、口译的标准

口译的任务是将一种语言形式转化成另一种语言形式，涉及两种或两种以上的语言。口译最基本的标准是"快""准""畅"。

（一）"快"

由于口译的时间性、现场性、即席性等因素，因而在翻译的过程中速度要快，节奏感要强。速度的快慢取决于口译员对原语的理解能力及目的语的表达能力。不管目的语是口译员的母语还是非母语，口译员对这两种语言都必须熟练掌握，运用自如。对语言掌握的熟练程度直接影响到口译的流利程度和速度。

（二）"准"

口译的另一个标准是准确。如果口译员只追求速度和流利程度而忽视了准确性，那么口译的质量就难以保证。所以，准确性在口译中是至关重要的，只有准确无误地将一方讲话的内容传递给另一方，才能真正达到口译的目的。因此，要做到快而准。口译准确的范围涉及内容（包括主题、论点等）、措辞、语法、语调等。高质量的口译应该是用另一种语言对说话者所说内容的再现，切忌篡改原意。

（三）"畅"

流利是口头表达的基本要求，也是口译的另一个重要标准。在口译中，"达"就是语言通达、通顺、流畅。口译要做到流利，一要"快"，二要"畅"。口译员必须迅速、及时地把一方的话语信息传达给另一方，做到语速流畅、节奏适当、反应敏捷、出口利落，而不能吞吞吐吐、慢条斯理。

易懂指口译的语言要口语化，简洁明快、直截了当，符合目的语的表达方式，使人一听就懂。特别是汉译英时，一定要避免汉语式的英语，或"对号入座"式的"死译"，不能让听者不知所云。

当然，快速、准确、流利的口译是建立在口译员对两种交际语言的技巧和文化知识熟练掌握及口译员快速反应基础之上的。因此，打好两种语言的基本功，加强口译实践锻炼是口译员获得良好口译能力的根本途径。

三、口译的策略

没有"策略"意识，就不会有成功的口译；如果"策略"判断错误，口译更不会成功。以下各项"策略"代表了具体的选择方向及其先后顺序。

（一）准备的方式

口译的事前准备关键在选定"准备范围"及事半功倍的"准备方式"。而做出正确判断的基准有以下几项因素：第一，了解口译的目的，配合口译的需求，圈定准备的范围；第二，了解讲话者处理信息的程序及方式（如是否使用幻灯片，或采取问答而非读稿的方式讲话），以决定准备的方式；第三，了解时间的紧迫程度，确定准备的优先级。接下来，口译员就可以决定是要专注于讲稿的准备，或是自行查阅相关数据，或者咨询委托人以获知更多的相关背景材料。

（二）辅助的安排

除了直接的准备工作之外，一些辅助性的安排也十分必要。例如，确认交替口译现场音箱的位置是否能让口译员听得清楚。如果不能，口译员应要求站在讲话者身边，而不是站在讲台的另一端。又如，有时委托人会让自己的工作人员前来协助译员，这时不妨让他坐在近处，碰到困难的时候，此人是最好的帮手。此外，在口译器材方面，务必要选择合适的耳机（最好自备），充分测试之后再行口译。

（三）表达的方式

在口译的表达方式上，有一部分应该是由口译员的经验来做判断的。例如，在交替口译方面，口译员的说话速度应根据传播理论视场地的大小而定，场地愈大、人愈多，语速应愈慢。此外，关于每一段话的长度，则应根据讲话者、口译员、听话者之间的人际互动而定，关系愈紧密，说话长度应愈短（最短可以一两句为一个口译段落）。此外，在用词的语体风格方面，从书面语的多少、句子的长度、语气词的使用等方面，都足以判断说话的风格正式（formal）与否。再者，如果在进行同声传译时，突然发生播放影片的情形，口译员无法边看影片边做同声传译的话，可以要求现场的讲话者边播影片边做讲述，口译员则是做间接的影片口译。

（四）技巧的选择

在口译过程中，由于现场的变量很多，因此必须运用不同的口译技巧。例如，是否做笔记，取决因素包括口译员对于主题的理解与专注的程度，或者有无另一位口译员可以代为笔记。又如，做同传带稿的视译，是否应首先进行部分笔译，这要取决于文稿修辞的精炼程度（如诗歌、广告），或是信息紧密的程度（并列的复合词超过 3 个）。此外，在进行即席问答的口译时，可运用"语篇分析"及"问答技巧"的要领，先指明提问的主题与应答的人，以便答复者有时间从容地思考。

（五）尽早与外宾沟通交流

要重视和外宾第一次见面和安排日程等活动。这种活动一般不涉及很深的技术内容。我们也可以把它看作是为以后正式口译所作的一种准备。首先，你可以通过这种初次见面，了解并逐渐适应外宾语音、语调。搞口译的人都知道，外国人的语音、语调也是五花八门。这就需要口译人员不仅能够听懂标准外语，而且要能够很快地适应各种地方音和不规范的外语。再者，通过初步接触，也能对谈判或讲话的内容有一些了解（在事前没有充分时间进行案头准备的情况下，这种了解尤为重要）。更为重要的是，这种初步接触可以消除临场紧张感，为下一步在正式场合进行口译做好心理准备。

此外，还有一种准备方式，效果很好。这就是和讲话人共同准备，商定讲话纲要。这实际上等于先打了一个草稿。有这样一些场合可以这样做：谈判时中方要提问题；宴会或其他比较正式场合可以预先准备讲话内容，如祝酒词等。

口译任务中最让人头疼的是讲话人事先准备了讲稿，照稿宣读，不理会口译员的工作，而口译员对这份讲稿事前又毫无准备，这实际上是在用口译方式做笔译工作。如果真是遇到这种情况，口译员当然也不能回避，只能靠其平时功力，沉着冷静，借助速记稿，尽可能转达讲话人的主要意思。

口译"策略"的运用与实务有关，只有通过大量口译实践活动，才能够学以致用。

四、口译的基础技巧

在口译技巧方面，我们以列表的方式来探讨 10 项"基础技巧"的训练目标、训练方法及适用的口译形式，如表 1-1 所示。表 1-1 右栏的口译形式：ST（sight translation）表示视译、CI（consecutive interpretation）表示接续口译、SI（simultaneous interpretation）表示同声传译。

表 1-1　口译基础技巧

基础技巧	训 练 目 标	训 练 方 法	适用口译形式
笔记技巧	运用笔记方法达成口译目的	1. 分析口译的笔记内容； 2. 笔记的符号与笔记方法	CI
跟读技巧	训练外语的流畅性与正确性	以边听边说的方式模仿外语的内容与节奏	CI/SI
顺译技巧	降低双语之间的干扰，提升口译的效率	1. 运用扩增及连贯技巧，依原文词序口译； 2. 运用顺译做带稿同声传译	ST/SI
数字口译技巧	熟悉英汉两种语言中数字的不同段位概念和分段方法	1. 数字互译时，要学会记录和分段； 2. 数字记录可采用各种简便符号或标点	ST/CI/SI
对译技巧	灵活运用已有的固定译词	讨论习语、名言、热门话题、专业词汇等的译词与译法	ST/CI/SI
重述练习	1. 外语的灵活运用能力； 2. 口语传达技巧	用同一外语将书面或口语的句子重组，但保持语意相同	ST/SI
全稿视译	将视译技巧灵活运用在不同形式的口译上	1. 讲者不说话，仅由口译员看稿视译； 2. 讲者全文念完，再由口译员视译； 3. 讲者宣读文稿，口译员同声口译； 4. 讲者跳读文稿，口译员同声口译	ST/CI/SI
缩减译法	用另一种语言精简地重组信息	以 5W1H（when，where，which，what，why，how）组成精简的新信息	CI
扩增译法	用另一种语言将信息稀释到听得清楚、说得明白的程度	1. 找长句的截断点加以分句； 2. 将语意浓缩的词加以扩增。	ST/SI
语篇分析	了解口语的语篇结构，培养预测下文的能力	1. 分析典礼致辞的语篇结构； 2. 熟记典礼致辞的常用套句	ST/CI/SI

口译的方法和技巧因其内容、要求、对象、场合的不同而不同。为了准确、完整地传达说话人的原意，口译员要根据具体情况，选择适当的方法，灵活运用各种不同的技巧，提高口译的表达效果。我们这里主要讨论基础阶段口译的五种技巧：笔记技巧、跟读技巧、顺译技巧、数字口译技巧、对译技巧（以习语为主）。

（一）笔记技巧

口译笔记（note-taking）技巧的训练是从事口译工作不可缺少的环节。口译训练主要就是技能培训，它训练学生通过分析、综合、推理和联想等方法学会在听辨原语语音的同时借助主题和认知知识进行分析、综合、推理，以正确理解听到的信息，并利用笔记帮助记忆和理解语篇意义，在讲话人完成一段讲话之后迅速、准确、完整地用目的语表达原语信息。口译笔记是辅助记忆的手段，是在倾听过程中用简单的文字或符号记下讲话内容中能刺激记忆的关键词。通过关键词能够提示译员讲话人所表述的意思，掌握其表述内容的前因后果及上下文的逻辑关系。除此之外，数字、地点、人名容易一听就忘，所以也要及时记下这些必要的细节。在口译过程中，笔记的开头和结尾是至关重要的，它关系到能否顺利完成口译任务。因此，开头和结尾绝对不能遗漏。记录第一句的目的是在发言人结束一段讲话后口译员能立即进入角色，开始翻译；记录最后一句是为了能够"有始有终"，让听讲人对前面的内容画个句号。至于段落内容的记录可以根据个人的情况而定，并不是记录得越多越好，记忆力好的口译员没有必要记录太多，记忆力不够好的译员可适当多记一些。

但是如果我们将精力完全集中在笔记上，而忽视了对摄入信息的分析理解和加工处理，那么笔记反倒会成为口译的绊脚石。所以，我们一定要遵从"记忆为主，笔记为辅"的基本原则，不能过分依赖笔记。

掌握了总体原则，接下来要考虑的自然是"怎样记笔记"这个战术问题了。"怎样记"是一个因人而异的问题，理论上以目的语加符号为宜，如"powerful country"记作"强□"，"我同意"记作"I√"，"观点、看法一致"记作"⊙ same"，"economic development"记作"经↑"等。用目的语记录能够帮助译员脱离原语的语言外壳，使笔记成为表达的雏形，为表达提供便利。不过理论归理论，遇到具体情况还应具体处理，口译员完全可以采用自己认为最迅速、最简短的方法进行记录。比如汉译英时，汉语是母语，用汉语记，自然反应更快，记得更准。相反，只要英文记录相对容易，就不必拘泥于上述的理论，束缚自己的手脚。还有英汉双语混用，也都是口译笔记个性化的体现。值得注意的是，无论用原语还是目的语，缩略语还是符号，关键是要能将记录下来的内容复原成完整准确的信息，千万不能造成识别的误区。

口译笔记的要点如下。

（1）少写多画。画线条比写文字快。线条形象，相当于翻译的"半成品"，有助于口译员眼看笔记，口出译文。以下两种情况下应该尽量用线条。

① 表示动作和动态的词句。比如，以上升的斜线代表"发展""增加""进步""进一步"；以下降的斜线代表"减少""下降""恶化"等。

② 表示因果或前后关系的词句。比如，用一条线代表"因为/所以""……之后""在……之前"，以体现出上下及前后之间的关联关系。

（2）少字多意。养成一个词的笔记不超过一个字的习惯。中文里有大量的词汇是由两个或两个以上的字组成。只要看到其中一个，你的短期记忆就应该能够补齐其余的字，不必多写。比如，"中国"最多写个"中"，"北京"最多写个"北"。英文单词也可同样处理。比如，"politics"最多写"poli"，"government"最多写"gov"，等等。另外，需要培养笔记与记忆互动，看到一个字能说出几个字，甚至一串词的能力。在有上下文的情况下，这不难。比如，谈中国的近况，听到"改革，开放"记一个"改"字，就不难从短期记忆中说出原文。听到"British Prime Minister Tony Blair"，记"PM"，也同样能说出原文。

（3）少线多指。通用一小组线条"／"标记，否则在自己本来熟悉的中英文之外，又编出一套自己不熟悉的文码使用，会导致需要想一想用哪个符号的情况，适得其反。

（4）少横多竖。采取从上往下的阶梯结构记录，尽量少用通常书写时的横向记录。阶梯结构形象地体现出上下文的逻辑结构，简化了口译员的思维过程，方便出译文。

（5）快速书写。必须发展自己的汉字快速书写系统。口译笔记完全是自己看，而且只需要几分钟之内能看懂就行。很多汉字笔画减少后，并不影响确认。我们这里讲的不是潦草，而是除了实际口译经常不得不潦草之外，花一些时间，把练习中或口译工作中常用的字琢磨一下，看看怎样减少笔画，或理顺笔画，一笔成字。

（6）明确结束。口译中，讲话人说一段，停下来让口译员译一段，然后再继续。这样，上一段话和下一段话之间，必须有明确的界限。上一次的结束点，就成了下一次口译的开始点。其重要性在于，如果笔记是从本子的 1/3 处开始的，下一段话可能写了 2 ～ 3 页，翻回来口译时，眼光无法确定这页上面哪一条线或符号是这次翻译内容的开始点，所以需要标明。

以下列举口译中的一个实例来说明口译笔记的一些基本要领。

讲话人：中国有一句话是这么说的，"上有天堂，下有苏杭"。这句话毫无夸张之意，苏杭这两座邻近上海的历史名城，以其秀丽的景色每年吸引了数以百万计的海内外游客。例如，中国南方园林建筑艺术之典范、迷人的苏州园林，在有限的空间里造就了无数的自然景观。园林的池塘、河水、石头、花朵、树木给游客带来了如诗般的意境，是赴苏州观光客的必游之地。

笔记： 中　saying："…"
　　　　 夸
　　　　 SZ、HZ 近 SH／历 city
　　　　　　＼　　　→
　　　　　 Beauty←Ms 中外旅°
　　　　 e. g：中 园 archi. 典
　　　　　　　　　　↙
　　　　　　　 SZ：（空）▲ landscape
　　　　　　　　 —　＝＝＝＝＝

池
河
石　　诗：must→ 观°
花
木

总之，记笔记是为了突出中心，提示难点，助短期记忆一臂之力，所以笔记的方法一定要得当。逐字逐句地记录既办不到，也没必要，而且还会分散精力影响听的效果。口译笔记应简短、清晰、易辨，寥寥几个关键词，能为理解后面的表达起到很好的提示作用。口译笔记有一定的规则可循，但又具有强烈的个性化，因此我们必须在反复练习的基础上，发展一套适合自身特点的笔记体系（参见 Appendix A），并在实践中不断完善，通过优化了的笔记系统提高口译质量。

（二）跟读技巧

跟读技巧即影子练习（shadow-exercise）。这种方法就是用同一种语言几乎同步地跟读原语发言人的讲话，它可以训练听说同步技巧和注意力的分配。刚开始训练时可以和原语同步开始，待操练了一段时间后，可以迟于原语片刻至一句话的时间跟读。跟读时耳朵、嘴巴和大脑要一起派上用场，耳朵听、嘴巴说、脑子记。这是需要精力非常集中的一种练习，也是提高语速、提高理解速度、纠正语音语调的最好方法。在高语速条件下，边跟读边完全理解语义是有相当难度的，但这种训练能为口译打下扎实的基础。各种新闻、谈话节目、研讨会、音乐体育节目、演讲等都是上好的训练材料。

另外，还可增加一些"干扰性"练习，譬如一边听、一边写一些不相关的内容，如数字、人名等，分散使用注意力，那样效果会更好。

下面举一例来进行说明。

> GAZA, Jan. 1 (Xinhua) — Nizar Rayan, one of the top Hamas leaders in the Gaza Strip was killed in an Israeli airstrike on Thursday afternoon, the Palestinian Hamas movement said in a statement sent to reporters.
>
> The statement said that the Israeli war planes carried out airstrikes against one of Rayan's house in northern Gaza Strip, killing the Hamas leader, his wife and eight of his children.
>
> Rayan is the top Hamas leader in northern Gaza Strip, and is among the most prominent Hamas leadership in all Gaza Strip.
>
> Meanwhile, according to Palestinian heath official, the death toll in the Israeli massive airstrikes on Gaza has reached 410, as the Israeli operation enters its sixth day.

跟读训练一般可以有以下两种方法。

（1）单纯做跟读训练，看看能不能完全跟下来。

（2）在完成跟读和干扰性训练之后，马上用原语概述所听到的原声录音的内容。

（三）顺译技巧

顺译（linear interpretation）就是按照原文的词序一个意群一个意群地去翻译，必要时做些"焊接"的工作。顺译的特点是快和口语化，适于口译和一般难度的笔译①。但顺译法并不是按照字的顺序一个接一个地去翻译，而是找出句子里"有意义"的意群，以意群为单

---

① 侯国金. 口译金话筒［M］. 大连：大连理工大学出版社，2003.

位进行翻译。所谓"有意义"的意群，指的是译员能够从原语中认知到讲话者的意思。顺译仅限于顺结构、顺词序的传译，是词词对应的顺译。至于意群的长短认定因人而异，因为每位口译员对于信息接收及处理的方法各有不同。一般来说，随着经验的累积，口译员可以接受较长的意群。顺译法对于口译员，尤其是初学者来说可以减轻不少的负担。

英汉两种语言在语序和词序上有很大的差异，顺译可以减轻记忆的压力，但是将切分开的意群在尽可能减少移位的前提下连贯起来则需要一定的技巧。在以下例句中，"/"表示断句处，"＋"表示补充信息，可以采用顺译法处理。

1. There are still 10 minutes/before we call it a day.

   还有 10 分钟，我们就下课。

2. My visit to China comes on an important anniversary，＋as the Vice President mentioned.

   我对中国的访问，正逢一个重要的周年纪念，这正如副主席刚才说的那样。

3. The conference will resume/at 6 p. m. /after the board has met privately.

   会议六点继续进行，董事会在此之前先要碰个头。

4. Prof. Smith asked us not to be afraid of mistakes/in practicing interpreting.

   史密斯教授叫我们不要害怕出错，尤其是在练习口译的时候。

5. Whatever the foreign media call me，＋either "China's Gorbachev" or "economic czar"，or anything else，I am not happy about that.

   对于外界称我为"中国的戈尔巴乔夫"也好，"经济沙皇"也好，我都不高兴。

6. Please allow me to say something/on behalf of/my colleagues of ABC Organization.

   请允许我说几句话，来代表我们 ABC 组织的同事们表达我们的心意。

7. The answer to the question of/whether we should continue to hold the meeting as planned depends in part on when the epidemic disease is curbed.

   问题的答案在于，我们是否可以继续按计划举行会议，部分地取决于什么时候那种传染病会得到控制。

以上各句的译文听起来虽然不是那么顺畅，但是在视译和同声传译等特定的场合却是口译员必不可少的翻译技能。

（四）数字口译技巧

数字口译（numerical interpretation）是口译中的一大难关，即使是资深口译员，当遇到数字时，尤其是遇到五位数以上的数字时，亦不敢有丝毫松懈。大多数口译员"闻数色变"，数字翻译已成为严重制约现场口译质量的"瓶颈"。这不仅仅因为数字难译，更因为在商贸谈判或外交活动中，数字误译所造成的后果是不堪设想的。如果说遇到难译的词语时，口译员还可以通过解译的方法绕道走，但数字的口译却无道可绕。

印欧语系诸语言与汉语互译时，存在着数字换算的"数级"差异，给数字口译带来很大的干扰和障碍。汉英计数的习惯不同，使用的基数单位不同，表达方式也不同。例如，汉语中"万"以上数字分成"十万""百万""千万""亿"等四位一组的进位组合单位，而英语却分成三位一组的进位组合单位。具体到最常见的汉英数字口译，碰到几千几百，还好处理，一旦过万，就极容易发生错译。

英语学习者都知道，英语数字的表达以每三位数为一段位，这与汉语以每四位数为一段位的表达方法完全不同。

英语数字分段法如下。

第一段位：	one	ten	hundred
第二段位：	thousand	ten thousand	hundred thousand
第三段位：	million	ten million	hundred million
第四段位：	billion	ten billion	hundred billion
第五段位：	trillion		

汉语数字分段法如下。

第一段位：	个	十	百	千
第二段位：	万	十万	百万	千万
第三段位：	亿	十亿	百亿	千亿
第四段位：	万亿	1	2	3

如果我们将英汉数字对照排列的话，就可以清楚地体会到英汉数字分段上的差异给口译员带来的困难。

1	one	一
10	ten	十
100	one hundred	一百
1, 000	one thousand	一千
10, 000	ten thousand	一万
100, 000	one hundred thousand	十万
1, 000, 000	one million	一百万
10, 000, 000	ten million	一千万
100, 000, 000	one hundred million	一亿
1, 000, 000, 000	one billion	十亿
10, 000, 000, 000	ten billion	一百亿
100, 000, 000, 000	one hundred billion	一千亿
1, 000, 000, 000, 000	one trillion	一万亿

诚然，数字的口译的确比较复杂、困难，但还是有一定的规律可循。口译员可根据具体情况采取以下做法。

1. 单纯数字口译练习

（1）熟练掌握汉英基本数字的读法规则。汉语是我们的母语，但许多人对大数字尤其是亿以上的数字的正确读法把握不准。对汉语的"天文数字"无法快速地反应并准确读出；而英语数字读法中连词 and 的位置，只出现在百位数和十位数之间，往往会被误读，从而暴露出英语地道程度的不到位。因此，熟读汉英数字是准确翻译数字的基础。

（2）做到整数一口清。要摸清汉英数字表达的规律，汉语有"个、十、百、千、万、十万、百万、千万、亿"，而英语只有"个、十、百、千、百万、十亿"等。汉语中的"万"和"亿"在英语中没有对应的表达法。"万"只能译作 ten thousand；"十万"译作 one hundred thousand；"亿"则译成 hundred million。要通过一定量的转换训练，熟练地将汉语的万、十万、千万、亿快速准确地换译成英语的十个千、一百个千、十个百万、一百个百万。只要持之以恒，久而久之，则熟能生巧，做到整数一口清。

（3）将烦琐的数字化简，分割记录。汉语数字表达可以从右至左每四位分成一组，如1890,3567,0250；英语数字表达法则是从右至左每三个分成一节，如189,035,670,250。口译时要学会使用"点三杠四"记录法。"点三"指逗号之间的三位数，"点"的作用如同"分节号"；而"杠四"则指斜杠之间有四位数字，即汉语的数字进位关系。听到数字，汉译英时，忽略"万"和"亿"等单位，把各位数字迅速准确地写下，再按英语数字进位规律从右至左每三个分成一节，如189,035,670,250。这样，在口译时只需照着逗号所提示的英语数字表达习惯读出即可：one hundred and eighty-nine billion, thirty-five million, six hundred and seventy thousand, two hundred and fifty。而英译汉时，则不管"billion""million""thousand"等单位，把各位数字迅速准确地写下，再按汉语数字进位规律从右至左每四位分成一节，如1890,3567,0250，然后按着逗号所分的三组用汉语数字表达习惯读出，即1890亿，3567万，零250。上述"分组割块"的数字速换法简单、方便、迅速、易辨。

2. 模糊数字的口译

在口译过程中，对模糊数字的译法也很重要。模糊数字在语言交际中经常出现，如"几个""十几个""几十个""成千上万个"等，这些模糊数字的表达法需要平时积累，熟记于心。我们来看看以下模糊数字的译法。

几个——several；a few；some

四五个——four or five

八九个——eight or nine

十几个——over a dozen；less/no more than twenty；more than ten

几十个——dozens of

几十年——decades

二十出头——a little/a bit over twenty

三十岁左右——thirty（years old）or so；about thirty（years old）

近七十岁了——almost/nearly seventy（years old）

八十好几了——well over eighty（years old）

七点左右——around seven o'clock

四天左右——four days or so

大约一里处——somewhere about one li

好几百——hundreds of

成千上万，千千万万——thousands of

几百万——millions of

几十亿——billions of

3. 分数、小数、百分数的口译

1）分数

分数是由基数词和序数词合成的，分子用基数词表示，分母用序数词表示。除了分子是"1"的情况外，序数词都要用复数形式。例如：

1/2—a (one) half	1/3—one third
2/3—two thirds	3/4—three quarters
7/12—seven twelfths	

比较复杂的分数如下：

20/87—twenty over eighty-seven	33/90—thirty-three over ninety
$2^{1/2}$—two and a half	$4^{2/3}$—four and two thirds

2）小数

表示小数时，小数点前面的基数词和前面讲的基数词的读法相同；小数点后的数字则必须一一读出。例如：

0.0089—（zero/naught）point zero zero eight nine   1.36—one point three six

3）百分数

百分数由 percent 表示，百分号％读作 percent，应用时常与 by 连用。例如：

0.68％—zero point six eight percent   6％—six percent

369％—three hundred and sixty nine percent

The price of cotton was reduced by 25 percent. 棉花的价格下降了25％。

（五）对译技巧（习语、引语的口译技巧）

习语（idiom）是语言中的特殊成分，是经过长期的使用而提炼出来的结构整齐、固定、语义生动、形象的短语或短句。英语习语包括俗语（colloquialisms）、谚语（proverbs）、俚语（slangs）等。引语属于人们的日常生活语言，包括人们喜欢引用的诗词名句、标语、谚语、人名、书名和典故等内容。

习语、引语的成功口译主要靠口译员两种语言的扎实功底，包括对两种语言的词汇、文学、文化背景知识的丰富积累和口译技巧的熟练掌握。

1. 习语的口译

形象点讲，习语的口译主要有4种方法：依样画葫芦、移花接木、添枝加叶和另起炉灶。翻译习语既要尽力保持原语的民族特色，又要符合译语的语言习惯，以不引起错误的联想为原则，同时还要保持习语的形式美及照顾到原习语的褒贬色彩。

1）依样画葫芦

依样画葫芦就是我们常说的"直译"，即照字面意思翻译。这种翻译一方面不失真，另一方面也为对方的语言增添了新鲜血液。例如：

英 语	汉 语
a gentleman's agreement	君子协定
a ray of hope	一线希望
castles in the air	空中楼阁
to fish in troubled water	浑水摸鱼
as light as a feather	轻如鸿毛
Honesty is the best policy.	诚实为上策。
in black and white	白纸黑字

汉 语	英 语
得寸进尺。	Give him an inch and he'll take an ell.
隔墙有耳。	Walls have ears.
冷言冷语	cold words
失败乃成功之母。	Failure is the mother of success.
事实胜于雄辩。	Facts speak louder than words.
血浓于水。	Blood is thicker than water.

2）移花接木

有些英语习语在汉语中能找到在内容、形式上都基本相同的对应习语，它们往往在意义和比喻上都很相似，口译时则可以套用汉语中的同义习语。例如：

an eye for an eye and a tooth for a tooth	以眼还眼，以牙还牙。
to cry up wine and sell vinegar	挂羊头卖狗肉
as poor as a church mouse	一贫如洗
a drop in the ocean	沧海一粟
at sixes and sevens	乱七八糟
to spend money like water	挥金如土
to kill two birds with one stone	一箭双雕

3）添枝加叶

因译语中找不到与原语相对应的表达法，译员需做补充说明，对原语加以解释或另加注释，以帮助译语读者理解其含义。这种方法尤其适用于一些典故和歇后语的翻译。

to meet one's Waterloo	遭遇惨败，一败涂地
He who fails to reach the Great Wall is not a true hero.	不到长城非好汉。
Achilles' heel	唯一致命弱点
a Pandora's box	潘多拉之盒，灾难、麻烦、祸害的根源

王小二过年——一年不如一年

Wang Xiao'er spending the New Year — one year is worse than another; like Wang Xiao'er's life, one year is worse than another

Note：Wang Xiao'er in Chinese can mean any poor fellow at the bottom of the society.

肉包子打狗——有去无回

Chasing a dog by throwing meat dumplings at it — gone, never to return

4）另起炉灶

当译语中难以找到与原文形象相同的习语来套用时，便可采用一种"另起炉灶"的翻译原则，即"意译"，因为这类习语在结构和字面意思上，英汉两种语言似乎无相近之处。

Rome was not built in a day.　　冰冻三尺，非一日之寒。

to hope that one's child will be somebody in the future　望子成龙

let the cat out of the bag　说走了嘴，露了马脚

to call a spade a spade　实话实说，直言不讳

to miss the boat　坐失良机

2. 引语的口译

引语的口译关键在于理解原语的意义，通常以意译的方式处理。对于引语的口译来说，平时积累至关重要。

下边是一些中外领导人演讲时常用的名人格言和经典佳句，配有英汉译文，可供口译学习者参考。

化干戈为玉帛。　beat swords into ploughs

欲穷千里目，更上一层楼。

We widen our views 3 hundred miles by ascending one flight of stairs.

会当凌绝顶，一览众山小。

When reaching the great peak (of Mount Tai), we hold all mountains in a single glance.

不到黄河心不死。Until all is over, ambition never dies.

路漫漫其修远兮，吾将上下而求索。

The way ahead is long; I see no ending; yet high and low I'll search with my will unbending.

同舟共济　Help one another, for we are all in the same boat.

天下为公　justice for all in the world

四海之内皆兄弟。　All men are brothers.

不管黑猫还是白猫，能抓到老鼠就是好猫。

Black cat or white cat：if it can catch mice, it's a good cat.

不登高山，不知天之高也；不临深渊，不知地之厚也。

One can never be aware of the height of the sky without climbing up a high mountain; nor the depth of the earth without looking down into a deep abyss.

大江东去，浪淘尽，千古风流人物。

The endless river eastward flows; with its huge waves are gone all those gallant heroes of bygone years.

但愿人长久，千里共婵娟。

We wish each other a long life so as to share the beauty of this graceful moonlight, even though miles apart.

二人同心，其利断金。

If two people are of the same mind, their sharpness can cut through metal.

苟利社稷，死生以之。

Life or death, I will do whatever I can for the benefits of the country.

俱往矣，数风流人物，还看今朝。

All are past and gone; we look to this age for truly great man.

民为贵，社稷次之，君为轻。

The people are the most important element in a state; next are the gods of land and grain; least is the ruler himself.

人有悲欢离合，月有阴晴圆缺，此事古难全。

People have sorrow and joy; they part and meet again. The moon dims or shines; it waxes or wanes. Nothing is perfect, not even in the olden days.

两情若是长久时，又岂在朝朝暮暮。

If love between both sides can last for aye, why need they stay together night and day?

Unit 2

Reception of Guests
待人接物

I. Objectives

After reading this unit, you are required to

☑ practice memory and note-taking techniques.

☑ get familiar with expressions related to reception of guests.

☑ present itinerary and reception techniques in English.

II. Vocabulary Work

1. receptionist　*n.*　接待员
2. schedule/itinerary　*n.*　日程安排
3. airsick　*a.*　晕机的
4. reservation　*n.*　预订
5. lobby　*n.*　前厅
6. registration　*n.*　登记
7. deposit　*n.*　定金
8. procedure　*n.*　手续，程序
9. suitcase　*n.*　小提箱
10. briefcase　*n.*　公文包
11. shower　*n.*　淋浴
12. bathtub　*n.*　浴缸
13. suite　*n.*　套间
14. deluxe　*a.*　豪华的
15. cabinet　*n.*　橱柜
16. wardrobe　*n.*　衣柜
17. corridor　*n.*　过道
18. lounge　*n.*　休息厅
19. attendant　*n.*　服务员
20. reception　*n.*　招待会
21. banquet　*n.*　宴会
22. feast　*n.*　盛宴
23. luncheon　*n.*　午宴
24. toast　*n.*　祝酒
25. treat　*v.*　款待，招待
26. hospitable　*n.*　好客的
27. speciality　*n.*　特色风味
28. tasty/delicious　*a.*　美味的
29. flavour　*n.*　风味，口味
30. dessert　*n.*　点心，甜食

III. Phrase Interpreting

A **From English to Chinese**

1. come all the way
2. a thoughtful arrangement
3. reception program
4. customs formalities
5. entry/exit/tourist visa
6. baggage claim area
7. terminal building
8. departure lounge

9. departure/arrival time   10. round-trip ticket

B **From Chinese to English**

1. 我非常荣幸地……   2. 免税商店
3. 旅客登记表   4. 国际礼节
5. 欢迎/告别宴会   6. 公务签证
7. 过境签证   8. 普通签证
9. 护照延期   10. 签发护照

IV. Sentence Interpreting

A **From English to Chinese**

1. There is an old Chinese saying that goes, "Isn't it a great joy to have friends from afar?"
2. On behalf of my company, I'd like to extend a warm welcome to you who have come all the way from Canada to Kunming.
3. If it is not too inconvenient, I wonder if a small change can be made in the schedule.
4. We are very grateful for the considerate services you've provided us during our stay here. We have had a very pleasant stay.
5. This visit has proved to be both enjoyable and very fruitful. We are looking forward to further cooperation with you.

B **From Chinese to English**

1. 坐了这么长时间的飞机，一路还好吧？
2. 请允许我介绍一下我的总经理王先生。他是专程从杭州赶回来和你会面的。
3. 如果你们有什么建议，请一定提出来，我们会尽量满足你们的要求。
4. 我知道大家明天的日程安排得很紧，就不多留你们了。希望大家今天晚上好好休息，再见。
5. 我代表我的同伴，感谢你们为我们做出的一切。我们来到这里以后，一直感受着你们最热烈的友谊与款待。你们对我们不仅敞开家门，热情相待，而且开诚布公，推心置腹。

V. Dialogue Interpreting

Directions: *Interpret the following conversation alternatively into English and Chinese.*

A： Mary, I'm planning a trip to Chicago and Denver, with Los Angeles as a final destination. I'd like you to make the necessary arrangements for me.

B： 好的，先生。您打算怎么走？

A： I'd like to go by train from here to Chicago and spend two days there. Then I'd like to fly to Denver for a stay of two nights. I want to go on to Los Angeles by plane for an indefinite stay of three or four days.

B： 我马上就和火车站及机场的接待员联系。您还是订卧铺票吗？

A： Yes. And please make sure the train has a club car and a dinner.

B： 您打算什么时候走？

A： I expect to depart for Chicago on Monday, May 6th, any time after 12:00 pm. I'll spend the evening of the 6th and all day the 7th there. I'll leave on the 8th, on either a late afternoon or an early evening flight for Denver. I want to be in Denver all day May 9th. I plan to leave for Los Angeles on an early morning flight on the 10th. Please book an open return flight from Los Angeles to New York.

B： 您还是订头等舱的票吗？我给您在哪儿预订酒店？

A： Yes, first class. I've been quite satisfied with the hotels I've used as lodging before in these cites. Please make reservation for me at those places. Get all the information together, and please report back to me as soon as possible.

 VI. Text Interpreting

Ⓐ From English to Chinese

Ladies and gentlemen,

Permit me first to thank you, our Chinese hosts, for your extraordinary arrangements and hospitality. My wife and I, as well as our entire party, are deeply grateful.

In the short period of six days, we have gone a longer distance than the world-renowned "Long March". We have acquired a keen sense of the diversity, dynamism, and progress of China under your policies of reform and opening to the outside world.

My wife and I have a special regard and personal friendship for the people of China. Beijing is for us an old and nostalgic home. During our stay here ten years ago we spent a great deal of memorable time with the people here — working, shopping, sightseeing, and touring the city on our bicycles. During that time we never experienced anything other than the utmost courtesy and genuine friendship of the Chinese people.

Those were happy days. They were good days, important days. We were part of the dramatic process which brought us back together and set us on the road to a genuine, friendly and cooperative relationship.

My visit is a symbol of the good faith, with which we seek to build up the strength of our friendship, our cultural and commercial ties and our important strategic relationship. Events of the past decade have confirmed time and time again that our friendship and cooperation will continue to flourish and yield more fruits in the days to come.

B **From Chinese to English**

女士们，先生们：

早上好！

首先，请允许我代表清华大学计算机科学系06级一班全体同学对各位表示最衷心的感谢。很长时间以来，我们一直期望见到你们。今天正是一个不错的日子。

现在，我简单地介绍一下我的学校，因为我想把最精彩的部分留给各位去挖掘。清华大学闻名国内外。假如你想遇见最令人敬仰的学者，请你来清华。假如你想遇见最勤奋刻苦的学生，请你来清华。假如你想发现最迷人的校园，请你来清华。我衷心希望各位在清华过得愉快。

谢谢各位！

VII. Enhancement Practice

1 Shadow-speaking in English 英语影子练习

Directions: *Listen to the MP3 and reiterate what you have heard simultaneously.*

Eastern China's Shandong Province held International Business Reception in Beijing Diaoyutai Hotel on Nov. 29th, 2004. About 170 guests attended the reception, including foreign ambassadors and envoys and commercial counselors to China, representatives from international organizations, multinational companies and chambers of commerce, officials of Chinese relevant ministries and committees, officials of the Government of Shandong Province, representatives from peninsular cities and famous enterprises of Shandong Province.

The reception, whose theme is "Friendship, Exchange, Cooperation and Development", introduced the investing environment of Shandong Province, aiming to further promote Shandong Province to the world. Mr. Han Yuqun, Governor of Shandong Province, made a welcoming speech at the reception. Mr. Sun shoupu, Vice Governor of Shandong Province, hosted the reception. Mr. Liangbo, Deputy Director General of Department of Foreign Trade and Economic Cooperation of Shandong Province, made a speech titled "Strengthening Cooperation for Development", introducing the investing environment of Shandong Province, key fields of its recent cooperation and effective measures taken to promote the development of Shandong peninsular manufacturing base.

At the reception, a picture exhibition of some famous enterprises of Shandong Province was also held.

Before the reception, Mr. Han Yuqun respectively met with Mr. Kim Ha Joong, ambassador of South Korean to China, Mr. Muziwakhe Themba Kubheka, ambassador of South Africa to China, Mr. Sandor Meszaros, ambassador of Hungary to China, envoys and counselors of Japan, Germany and other countries to China, Mr. Liang Baorong, Director of Hong Kong Special Administrative Region Beijing office, representatives from such multinational companies such as Nokia, Lucent and Shell. They exchanged views on further strengthening communication and cooperation in the future.

2　Memory & Note-taking 记忆、笔记练习

A English Passage Retelling

Directions: *This part is to test your short-term memory and note-taking skills. You are required to repeat what you have heard from the recording. You may take notes while you're listening. This passage will be played only once.*

World Expo' 2010 Shanghai

China owes its successful bid for the World Exposition in 2010 to the international community's support for and confidence in its reform and opening-up. The World Exposition will be the first one in a developing country since it was first held in 1851 in London, UK, which gives expression to the expectations the world's people place on China's future development.

The theme of World Expo 2010 Shanghai is "Better City, Better Life". The prospect of future urban life, a subject of global interest, concerns every nation and its people. Being the first World Exposition on the theme of city, Expo 2010 will attract about 200 nations and international organizations to participate in it, with an estimate of 70 million visitors from home and abroad.

B Chinese Passage Retelling

Directions: *This part is to test your short-term memory and note-taking skills. You are required to repeat what you have heard from the recording. You may take notes while you're listening. This passage will be played only once.*

上海旅游的世界之最

上海作为中国一个现代化的城市，其影响力是非常大的。它不仅在国内，就在国际上也是比较有知名度的，它有着许多世界之最或是亚洲之最，足以让我们为它感到骄傲和自豪。而作为一个生活在如此现代化城市的居民来说，就应该要认识上海、了解上海，那么就来看看上海的世界和亚洲之最吧。

上海是世界摩天大楼榜席位最多的城市，现有 1700 座，在建及规划 1500 座，累计 3200 座，首次超过纽约。

上海有世界最大的城市规划模型：上海城市规划馆，上海内环线全景。

上海有世界最大的，主跨最大、最长，螺旋最大的钢拱桥：卢浦大桥。

上海有世界最长、最宽的跨海大桥：东海大桥。

上海有世界最大的陆运枢纽：上海南站。

上海有世界陆上速度最高的运输工具：磁悬浮列车。

上海有世界造价最高，设施最先进，包含世界最大汉字"上"字跑道的专业 F1 赛道。

上海有世界最大的深水港：洋山深水港。

上海是亚洲环城高架最多的城市：上海外环线、中环线、内环线。

3 Numerals 数字听译练习

A 单纯数字听译练习

202	234	1,234	1,031	1,150
11,234	155,721	6,155,702	26,000,008	326,414,718
4,302,000,000	1/2	1/3	1/8	1/4
2/3	$1\frac{5}{9}$	317/509	0.5	0.25
0.125	93.64 m	2′15.11″	15℃	32℉
0℃	−5℃			

B 带有数字的句子听译练习

1. 北京共辖 14 个区、2 个县，全市面积 16 801.25 平方千米。
2. 中南大学现占地面积 380 万平方米，校舍总建筑面积 233 万平方米。
3. 在中国工作的外国人已达到 986 000 人。
4. 2008 年，该公司有 53 328 平方米的建筑竣工。
5. 明年将有 596 万大学生毕业。

4　Idioms Interpreting 习语口译练习

A From English to Chinese

1. Facts speak louder than words.　　2. Failure is the mother of success.
3. Honesty is the best policy.　　4. to be armed to the teeth
5. to pick bones from an egg　　6. Soon learnt, soon forgotten.
7. Spare the rod, spoil the child.　　8. Years bring wisdom.
9. Speech is the picture of the mind.
10. You can fool some of the people all the time, and all of the people some of the time; but you can't fool all of the people all the time.

B From Chinese to English

1. 一心一意。　　2. 沧海一滴。　　3. 轻如鸿毛。　　4. 实事求是。
5. 一见如故。　　6. 同甘共苦。　　7. 掩耳盗铃。　　8. 知识就是力量。
9. 一寸光阴一寸金，寸金难买寸光阴。　　10. 一回生，两回熟。

5　Linear Interpreting for Sentences 句子顺译练习

A From English to Chinese

1. I hope you will enjoy your stay with us in this hotel.
2. Would you like to have any wine with your dinner?
3. Service hours are: 7:00 a.m. to 9:00 a.m. for breakfast, 11:30 a. m. to 1:30 p.m. for lunch, 6:30 p.m. to 8:30 p.m. for dinner.
4. Allow me first of all to thank you, our host, for your extraordinary arrangements and hospitality.
5. Let me propose a toast to the health of our guests! Cheers!

B From Chinese to English

1. 他们每年可享受 30 天的带薪假期。
2. 有什么能为您效劳的?
3. 请问盥洗室在哪儿?
   在大厅靠近大门处。
4. 您能告诉我您的名字与房间号吗?
5. 请别遗忘您的东西。再见，谢谢您的光临。

6 Sight Interpreting for Passages 段落视译练习

A From English to Chinese

Distinguished Guests, Ladies and Gentlemen,

Thank you very much for your gracious welcoming speech. China is one of the earliest cradles of civilization and the visit to this ancient nation has long been my dream. This visit will give me an excellent opportunity to meet old friends and establish new contacts. I wish to say again that I am so delighted and privileged to visit your great country and this lovely town. I am deeply grateful for everything you have done for me since my arrival in China.

As an American manager of Sino-American joint venture for two years, I have to say that there are differences in business management between Chinese and Americans. We are more direct and straightforward than most Chinese colleagues due to our different cultural traditions. I can't say our way of doing business is absolutely superior. After all, there are strong points and weak points in both types of management. In recent years, more and more American business executives have recognized the strong points of the more humane way of Chinese management.

It is with great pleasure to exchange views and information, and reach common ground here. And I wish to share with you my thoughts on this topic in the further days. Thank you!

B From Chinese to English

女士们，先生们：

欢迎各位来我班参加我们的晚会。首先，请让我谈谈我的班级。我班有 50 名学生：26 名男生，24 名女生。我们大部分同学来自北京，大都年龄相同，17 岁。有的同学喜爱运动，有的则对读书感兴趣。我们共有 6 门课，包括英语、语文和数学。我们都喜欢英语，而且经常花很多时间学英语。

今晚的节目有短剧、小组合唱等，希望各位喜欢并玩得开心。谢谢。

Unit 3

Campus Life
校园生活

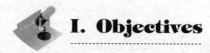

I. Objectives

After reading this unit, you are required to

☑ practice memory and note-taking techniques.

☑ get familiar with expressions related to campus life.

☑ interpret heated topics on campus in English.

II. Vocabulary Work

1. admission *n.* 允许进入，入学许可	16. stipend/subsidy *n.* 助学金
2. registration *n.* 注册	17. faculty *n.* 全体教职员工
3. major *n./v.* 主修	18. lecturer/instructor *n.* 讲师
4. minor *n./v.* 副修	19. commoner *n.* 自费生
5. course/curriculum *n.* 课程	20. boarder *n.* 寄宿生
6. mark/grade *n./v.* 分数	21. undergraduate *n.* 大学肄业生
7. assignment *n.* 课外作业	22. intern *n.* 实习生
8. term/semester *n.* 学期	23. graduate *n.* 毕业生
9. speciality/major *n.* 专业	24. club *n.* 学生俱乐部
10. supervisor *n.* 论文导师	25. society *n.* 学生社团
11. certificate *n.* 证书，证明文件	26. laboratory/lab *n.* 实验室
12. diploma *n.* 文凭	27. dormitory/dorm *n.* 宿舍
13. credit *n.* 学分	28. accommodation *n.* 住宿
14. tuition (fee) *n.* 学费	29. reward *n./v.* 奖励
15. scholarship *n.* 奖学金	30. cafeteria *n.* 自助小餐厅

III. Phrase Interpreting

Ⓐ From English to Chinese

1. academic year

2. core curriculum

3. required/compulsory course

4. optional/elective course

5. extracurricular activities

6. social practice

7. school report; report card

8. academic record; school record

9. academic activities　　　　10. campus culture

B **From Chinese to English**

1. 教学楼，教室楼　　　　　2. 大教室，阶梯教室
3. 行政办公楼　　　　　　　4. 学生会
5. 教员休息室　　　　　　　6. 专任教师
7. 高等学校　　　　　　　　8. 教育部
9. 教学大纲　　　　　　　　10. 毕业典礼

IV. Sentence Interpreting

A **From English to Chinese**

1. Nowadays, many students always feel cheerful at the mere mention of the coming life of high school or college they will begin. Unfortunately, for most young people, it is not a pleasant experience on their first day on campus.

2. A proper part-time job does not occupy students' too much time. In fact, it is unhealthy for them to spend all of time on their study. As an old saying goes: All work and no play makes Jack a dull boy.

3. The majority of students believe that part-time job will provide them with more opportunities to develop their interpersonal skills, which may put them in a favorable position in the future job markets.

4. A large number of people tend to live under the illusion that they had completed their education when they finished their schooling. Obviously, they seem to fail to take into account the basic fact that a person's education is a most important aspect of his life.

5. Our college greatly values our exchange relations with overseas institutions. Our exchange programs involve institutions in Germany, the United States, France, Japan and South Korea, and the annual exchanges of visits.

B **From Chinese to English**

1. 劳驾，你能告诉我学校图书馆在哪里吗?
2. 我们学校经常举行各种英语活动，诸如歌咏比赛、朗诵比赛、话剧演出等。
3. 中级口译课是只给英语系二年级学生开设的选修课。
4. 由于我在班级名列前茅，所以我连续四年获得大学奖学金。
5. 在各州和各地区，学校主要分为政府办和民办两大类。约三分之二的儿童上政府办的学校，这类学校是免费的。

V. Dialogue Interpreting

Directions：*Interpret the following conversation alternatively into English and Chinese.*

A： Patrick, I've been learning English for a long time. And I still can't speak good English. I've got really disheartened.

B： 慢慢来，杰克。毕竟冰冻三尺非一日之寒。

A： Can you make some suggestions?

B： 好的。英语是一种国际语言，它非常重要。可也像任何事情一样，在说好它之前你需要大量的练习。

A： How?

B： 我给你举个例子吧。你知道当人们学开车的时候，他们会犯很多错误。在该刹车的时候他们可能会踩油门。可那很正常，每个人都犯这种错误。

A： I know what you mean.

B： 学英语就像开车一样，你需要做的就是练习，别怕犯错。你犯的错误越多，就能快点说好英语。

A： It's easy to say, but hard to do.

B： 别着急啊。我会帮你的。请记住语言不仅仅是单词加语法，文化背景也很重要。

A： Jesus. What could I do before I can speak good English?

B： 和我练习就好了。我不是神，可我肯定能帮你学好英语。

VI. Text Interpreting

A From English to Chinese

Faced with a tough job market, fresh graduates are dreaming of running their own businesses instead.

But a recent survey has showed that such ambitions lack the required support and remain just that — dreams.

The Shanghai Municipal Employment Promotion Center poll of 1,276 graduates in several universities and colleges in the city, released last Friday, showed 59.78 percent of respondents considered the possibility of setting up a company or at least a small store.

"But they just stop at the 'thinking' stage," it stated.

Respondents put the top reasons for not going it alone down to a shortage of investment and a lack of business opportunity.

They also listed lack of business experience and social networks, the need for advanced study and objections from family members as factors that stood in their way.

More than 90 percent of the interviewees said they would rather take up a job after graduating and then consider starting their own business two or three years down the road.

Guo Bing, a senior student in Shanghai International Studies University majoring in English, decided he wanted to be his own boss last year.

But he is looking for a job first. "If I fail to find a satisfying job, I would like to establish a company in exhibition services," Guo said.

The Shanghai native has some relatives working in a local printing plant.

With their help, Guo hopes to produce exhibition brochures at a relatively low price. He is also confident that his English language skills can help him do well in the industry.

"Social networking is an important factor leading to business success," Guo said.

Guo said that the shortage of graduate jobs is the main reason driving more university students to set up a business right after their graduation.

The parents of university graduates are more willing to help their children start up alone, the survey showed.

"Once you win the support of your family, you have won half the battle," Guo added.

B **From Chinese to English**

上海大学有三个校区，校园占地 200 余万平方米。图书馆建筑面积 6.4 万平方米，馆藏图书 340 万册，期刊 3 600 余种，包括外文期刊 530 余种，网络和光盘数据库 60 余种。学校还建成了一批先进的基础教学实验中心、多媒体教室和体育场馆。校园通信光缆连接三个校区。

上海大学是上海市重要的人才培养基地。现有普通高校学生 43 000 余人，其中本科生 28 000 余人，研究生近 8 000 人，高职生近 7 000 人。另外，还有成人教育学生 10 000 余人。

VII. Enhancement Practice

1 Shadow-speaking in English 英语影子练习

Directions: *Listen to the MP3 and reiterate what you have heard simultaneously.*

WINTER vacation is no longer simply a time for family feasts and reunions with friends. It has become an important opportunity for college students to complete work internships.

Peng Hongmei, a junior English major from Southwest University in Chongqing, is searching for an internship at a private English training center in her city for the coming one-month vacation.

"I hope to gain some teaching experience before facing job interviews next year," said the 20-year-old girl, who hopes to become an English teacher in the future.

According to Peng, it's better to start job preparations as early as possible, "Next year I'll be too busy for internships and I'll have to start looking for jobs during the summer vacation."

As students across the country join Peng in search of a winter internship, both domestic and foreign companies are offering more positions.

2　Memory & Note-taking 记忆、笔记练习

Ⓐ English Passage Retelling

Directions： *This part is to test your short-term memory and note-taking skills. You are required to repeat what you have heard from the recording. You may take notes while you're listening. This passage will be played only once.*

A Speech

On behalf of Oxford University, I would like to thank you for all you have done for us. Ever since we arrived, we have been enjoying nothing but the warmest friendship and hospitality. You have opened your hearts as well as your homes to us. While our stay has been very short, we feel that it has been very rewarding, not only professionally, but in making new friends and broadening the channels of contact.

I would like to conclude with the hope that all of you will have a chance to come to the United States very soon, not only to continue our common pursuits of professional interest, but to partake our hospitality as well.

Finally allow me to propose a toast to the health and happiness of all the ladies and gentlemen present here.

Ⓑ Chinese Passage Retelling

Directions： *This part is to test your short-term memory and note-taking skills. You are required to repeat what you have heard from the recording. You may take notes while you're listening. This passage will be played only once.*

学 校 特 色

一、学生管理德育为先、严格规范

学校注重学生的习惯养成教育，大力开展德育教育，通过开展形式多样的活动培养学生的综合素质，校园文化生活丰富多彩。同时，学校严格实行封闭式管理，实行班主任跟班负责制，学生生活费由班主任管理，由班主任每周按时定额发放，培养学生良好的消费习惯。

二、教学管理突出技能、注重实用

学校非常注重学生实际动手能力的培养，充分利用先进的教学设施，将教学实践活动的各个环节贯穿于学生在校学习的全过程，每个专业设置了 5 ～ 6 门的实训课，确保学生进行专业技能操作实训的时间。学校将"双证制"纳入教学计划，要求学生在取得毕业证的同时，还必须考取相关的职业资格证书。

三、生活后勤条件优越、服务优质

学校各类生活设施齐全。教室装有电视机、饮水机，寝室配有程控电话，生活服务中心的食堂、超市、医务室实行一卡通的微机联网管理，为同学们提供质优价廉的服务。学校有 400 米的标准运动场及篮球场、网球场、羽毛球场、乒乓球场等，带给同学们丰富多彩的校园生活。

四、实习就业渠道畅通、安置到位

推行"订单式"培养的校企合作机制。我校与 100 多家国内外知名企业建立了"校企合作"关系，签订了订单培养协议，建立长期的人才供需关系。

3 Numerals 数字听译练习

Ⓐ 单纯数字听译练习

Country	Area（km²）	Population
Albania	28, 748	3, 180, 000
Austria	83, 871	8, 375, 300
Belarus	207, 600	9, 671, 000
Belgium	33, 990	10, 667, 000
Bulgaria	111, 001. 9	7, 560, 000
Croatia	56, 594	4, 435, 000
Cyprus	9, 251	791, 700
Czech Rep.	78, 866	10, 500, 000

| Denmark | 43,096 | 5,530,000 |

B 带有数字的句子听译练习

1. The total number of accidents fluctuated quite a lot during the period of 1982 – 2007.

2. If you look at the table, you can see that in 1982 the figure was 360,000, while in 1997, it had fallen to 313,000.

3. The best year in the period of 1992 – 2008 was 2006 when it stood at 332,000, after which it rose to a new peak of slightly under 360,000 in 2007.

4. We can see that from 2001 to 2007 there was a steady fall in the number of road accidents.

5. In China, Buddhism has a history of 2,000 years, Taoism over 1,700 years, and Islam over 1,300 years, while Catholicism and Protestantism became widespread in China primarily after the Opium War.

4 Idioms Interpreting 习语口译练习

A From English to Chinese

1. Love me, love my dog.
2. Seeing is believing.
3. Worse off than some, better off than many.
4. What is done cannot be undone.
5. Smooth water runs deep.
6. One man makes a chair and another man sits in it.
7. Rain before seven; fine before eleven.
8. Other men live to eat, while I eat to live.
9. Opportunity seldom knocks twice.
10. Not pleased by external gains, not saddened by personal losses.

B From Chinese to English

1. 青年人向前看，老年人向后看。
2. 是骡子是马拉出去遛遛。
3. 弱者等待机会，强者创造机会。
4. 人生非为己。
5. 良好开端，功成一半。
6. 青年冒失莽撞；成年发奋图强；老年遗憾懊丧。
7. 衣食足，知荣辱。
8. 真相总会大白。

9. 行路踏实，言谈深刻，饮酒豪爽，睡眠酣畅。
10. 大事化小，小事化了。

5 Linear Interpreting for Sentences 句子顺译练习

A From English to Chinese

1. I'd like to thank you for your presence at the party, and wish everyone good health and the very best of luck in everything in the New Year.
2. I hope this party will give us an opportunity to get to know each other better in a less formal way and to increase personal friendships.
3. The party was perfectly organized and I enjoyed every minute of it. And I am very grateful for this nice arrangement.
4. I would like to toast with you to this happy occasion at the close of the year.
5. May I hereby declare open "Shanghai International Symposium on Social Work"!

B From Chinese to English

1. 这个学校里所有的人都在一个餐厅吃饭。
2. 我们以前在同一个办公室工作，但我三年前就离开那儿了。
3. 我们通过广播、电视宣传我们厂的产品。
4. 他推荐汤姆到那个学校当教师。
5. 我决心把英语学得更好。

6 Sight Interpreting for Passages 段落视译练习

A From English to Chinese

Children

Today, the majority of kindergarten children in China are only-children. They are usually intellectually alert, eager to learn, and full of imagination and energy. On the other hand, they're egocentric, undisciplined, and lack self-control. Therefore, our education program stresses collectivism, mutual help and love. Children are encouraged to look after themselves. They are also taught the benefits of sharing. A study of the behavior of 1,000 kindergarten and primary school children showed that only-children aged 4 to 6 in both urban and rural areas are egocentric, while children with siblings exhibit the positive social behaviors of cooperation. But the only-children aged 9 to 10 show the positive qualities of behavioral and frustration control. This indicated the importance of a kindergarten education, which teaches children discipline and cooperativeness.

B From Chinese to English

我感谢哈佛大学陆登庭校长的邀请，使我有机会在这美好的金秋时节，来到你们这座美国古老而又现代化的学府。

哈佛建校 360 年来，培养出许多杰出的政治家、科学家、文学家和企业家，曾出过 6 位美国总统，30 多位诺贝尔奖获得者。先有哈佛，后有美利坚合众国，这说明了哈佛在美国历史上的地位。哈佛是最早接受中国留学生的美国大学之一。中国教育界、科学界、文化界一直同哈佛大学保持着学术交流。哈佛为增进中美两国人民的相互了解做出了有益的贡献。

Unit 4

Sightseeing & Travelling
观光旅游

I. Objectives

After reading this unit, you are required to

☑ practice memory and note-taking techniques.

☑ master the basic words and expressions about sightseeing and travelling.

☑ know some cultural background knowledge about business travel.

☑ find ways to improve your interpreting skills and performance.

II. Vocabulary Work

1. hike *n./v.* 徒步旅行	16. temple *n.* 寺庙
2. cruise *n./v.* 巡航，巡游	17. altar *n.* 坛
3. destination *n.* 目的地	18. pavilion *n.* 亭
4. itinerary *n.* 旅程，旅行计划	19. terrace *n.* 台
5. sightseeing *n.* 观光，游览	20. corridor *n.* 廊
6. cancellation *n.* 取消预定	21. castle *n.* 城堡
7. accommodation *n.* 住宿	22. marvelous *a.* 令人惊叹的，非凡的
8. motel *n.* 汽车旅馆	23. splendor *n.* 壮丽，壮观，辉煌
9. inn *n.* 旅馆，饭店	24. spectacular *a.* 壮观的，壮丽的
10. air-bridge *n.* 旅客桥	25. folklore *n.* 民俗风情
11. sunrise *n.* 日出	26. artifact/handicraft *n.* 手工艺品
12. sunset *n.* 日落	27. receipt *n.* 收据
13. statue *n.* 雕像	28. invoice *n.* 发票
14. spectacle *n.* 景象	29. exchange *n./v.* 兑换
15. landscape *n.* 风景，景色	30. complain *v.* 投诉

III. Phrase Interpreting

A **From English to Chinese**

1. tourist attraction/scenic spot
2. natural splendor/attraction
3. summer resort
4. national park
5. holiday resort
6. guided coach trip

7. peak season   8. off season

9. famous mountains and great rivers   10. sightseeing bus

B From Chinese to English

1. 丝绸之路   2. 佛教名山

3. 园林建筑   4. 诱人景色

5. 山清水秀   6. 湖石假山

7. 湖光山色   8. 依山傍水

9. 商务旅行   10. 套餐游，随团游

 IV. Sentence Interpreting

A From English to Chinese

1. Thank you very much for giving me such an excellent opportunity to visit this beautiful city and work with you.

2. I am honored to accompany you throughout your travel here. I will be glad if I can answer some of your questions now and address the others as we tour.

3. We have a tight schedule for your short visit. I hope you don't mind.

4. Would you please give me seven five-pound notes, four pound notes and four ten-shilling notes, and the rest in small change?

5. To come to China, one of the early cradles of civilization, has long been my dream and therefore, I feel very honored to be your guest.

B From Chinese to English

1. 你们能否提供这些：我们需要为30名游客预订从8月1号到8月5号接连五个晚上的15个双人房间，其中美式早餐也包括在房费中。

2. 这座古代的寺庙历史悠久，可追溯到初唐时期。

3. 苏州市有江南规模最大、最负盛名的园林。

4. 我想把我们旅游的一些特别注意事项向各位游客通告一下。

5. 这些节目集观光、度假和文化活动于一体，使游客有机会了解中国文化，尽情观赏所游之地的风土人情，尤其是当地的历史名胜和人文景观。

 V. Dialogue Interpreting

Directions：*Interpret the following conversation alternatively into English and Chinese.*

Sightseeing in Beijing

A： 我只是在北京作短暂的停留。我肯定要去参观长城，但我还有什么别的可以做呢？

B： Well, the Forbidden City is also a "must-see". It will really give you a sense of how magnificent ancient Chinese culture was.

A： 那要花多长时间呢？

B： I have been there countless times and can still spend a whole day, but if you are on a tight schedule, I would leave two hours minimum.

A： 那还有些什么我不该错过的呢？

B： I always recommend a pedicab ride through a hutong. You can do this as soon as you exit the Forbidden City. It will give you a real glimpse into a Chinese way of life that is quickly disappearing!

A： 太棒了，我真的很想去看看。哦，我还想去买些东西，我该怎么安排呢？

B： The Pearl Market is right across from the Temple of Heaven. There is a new subway line that stops there. First, visit the Temple of Heaven, then swing across the street for some quick souvenir shopping. Remember to bargain hard!

A： 好啊，这里的地铁好找吗？

B： No, not at all. It's clearly marked and stops are announced in English and Chinese. It's also a real time-saver.

A： 清楚了，最后还有什么建议吗？

B： You can't leave Beijing without trying some delicious local food. Be adventurous! Pop into any restaurant that looks interesting and order something.

A： 他们听得懂英语吗？

B： A lot of restaurants have added English or photos to their menus. There is usually someone who will be able to help you out. Even if no one can speak English, it is no problem to point to a dish on someone else's table. Chinese people are proud of their food culture and eager to share it. Don't be surprised if you even get invited to join someone for lunch!

A： 哇！真有趣！太棒了！你真的帮了我大忙。北京真是太大了，有太多东西玩了，真有点儿让人应接不暇！真的太谢谢你了！

B： My pleasure! Enjoy yourself in Beijing! It's really an amazing city and a great place to have an adventure!

VI. Text Interpreting

A From English to Chinese

Spotlight on Copenhagen

Are you too old for fairy tales? If you think so, Copenhagen is sure to change your mind.

See the city first from the water. In the harbor sits Denmark's best-known landmark: the Little Mermaid. Remember her? She left the world of the Sea People in search of a human soul in one of Hans Christian Andersen's beloved fantasies. From the harbor you can get a feel for the attractive "city of green spires". At twilight or in cloudy weather, the copper-covered spires of old castles and churches lend the city a dream-like atmosphere. You'll think you've stepped into a watercolor painting.

Copenhagen is a city on a human scale. You don't have to hurry to walk the city's center in less than an hour. Exploring it will take much longer. But that's easy. Copenhagen was the first city to declare a street for pedestrians only. The city has less traffic noise and pollution than any other European capital.

B From Chinese to English

您下一次去度假，考虑放弃老一套的旅游方式吗？如果您这样做了，那么，您应该就是许多正在享受较新的生态旅游模式的人们之一。正如它的名字所暗示那样，生态旅游重点是在保护生态，保护名胜古迹和自然遗产。另外，生态旅游以本土文化为特色，想方设法让当地社区管理并维护其资源。

过去，度假的人们总是把时间耗在大城市，如纽约、巴黎和东京的豪华宾馆里和参观都市著名的景点和博物馆上。还有一些人则喜欢去风景如画的夏威夷海滩放松自己，或是登上阳光明媚的加勒比海的游艇去散散心。他们很少与当地人进行交流互动，游客过分拥挤常常糟蹋了热门度假景点的自然美景。而且，过度的商业化使许多旅游点变成了旅游陷阱。

因此，自20世纪80年代初期以来，以探险为导向和以自然为基础的度假活动已逐渐地流行起来。伴随着全球环境意识的崛起和对文化多样化的尊重，生态旅游成为旅游观光产业中发展最快的一个组成部分。人们去喜马拉雅山脉翻山越岭，去荒野探险过简陋的生活，去亚马孙河热带雨林艰苦跋涉，去公海领略鲸鱼。跟住在城市舒服的五星级宾馆或是高级酒店相比较而言，这些都是具有诱惑力的选择。

 VII. Enhancement Practice

1　Shadow-speaking in English 英语影子练习

Directions：*Listen to the MP3 and reiterate what you have heard simultaneously.*

Lijiang—An Ancient Town in China

It is said there is a fairyland beneath the colorful clouds of southern China, a place blessed with fresh air, clear streams, breathtaking snow-capped mountains, and an undisturbed landscape inhabited by a friendly group of people. Life in this fairyland is so peaceful, a fairyland called Lijiang, located at the hub of Tibet, Yunnan and Sichuan provinces.

Around Lijiang, there are a number of splendid natural beauty spots that will certainly astonish you. If you like to see superlative natural scenery, Jade Dragon Snow Mountain which provides a majestic backdrop to the Moon-Embracing Pavilion at Black Dragon Pond will fulfill your desire. For those seeking an exotic experience in Lijiang, a visit to the Mosuo People beside Lugu Lake is a must. They are called the last "Kingdom of Women" on earth. If you would like to experience the local lifestyle, then come and participate in one or more of their various festivals that are held throughout the year.

2　Memory & Note-taking 记忆、笔记练习

Ⓐ **English Passage Retelling**

Directions：*This part is to test your short-term memory and note-taking skills. You are required to repeat what you have heard from the recording. You may take notes while you're listening. This passage will be played only once.*

Tourist Market

Thanks to its rich tourist resources — high mountains, elegant rivers, springs and waterfalls, rich and varied folk customs, rare species, scenic spots and historical sites, distinctive opera, music and dance, and world-famous cuisine — China attracts a large number of domestic and foreign tourists every year.

Today, China has one of the world's largest domestic tourist markets and an outbound market growing at a rate unequalled anywhere. In 2004, the incoming tourists reached 109. 038 million person-times, 19 percent up on 2003; foreign exchange revenue from tourism reached US$ 25. 74 billion, a 47. 8 percent year-on-year increase; the number of tourists from the 16 main source countries hit a record level, far surpassing the 2003 total.

China is emerging as the country with the world's highest growth rate for outbound tourism. According to a survey conducted by an international tourism monitoring agency of Asia-Pacific region, the average daily expenses (excluding purchases) of a Chinese tourist during one long holiday amounts to US$175; a German Chamber of Commerce survey shows average daily expenses of US$110 in Germany, second to American tourists' US$117; the Swiss Information Network report puts the figure for Switzerland at US$313, the highest spending for any source country.

B **Chinese Passage Retelling**

Directions：*This part is to test your short-term memory and note-taking skills. You are required to repeat what you have heard from the recording. You may take notes while you're listening. This passage will be played only once.*

北京市简介

北京简称京，是中国的首都，全国的政治、文化中心和国际交往的枢纽，也是一座著名的历史文化名城，与西安、洛阳、开封、南京、杭州并列为中国六大古都。

自然状况

北京位于华北平原西北边缘，市中心位于北纬39度，东经116度，四周被河北省围着，东南和天津市相接。全市面积一万六千多平方公里，辖16区（东城区、西城区、朝阳区、海淀区、丰台区、石景山区、门头沟区、房山区、通州区、顺义区、昌平区、大兴区、怀柔区、平谷区、密云区、延庆区），人口2,100余万。北京为暖温带半湿润大陆性季风气候，夏季炎热多雨，冬季寒冷干燥，春、秋短促，年平均气温10～12摄氏度。

古都历史

北京是世界历史文化名城和古都之一。早在七十万年前，北京周口店地区就出现了原始人群部落"北京人"。而北京建城也已有两千多年的历史，最初见于记载的名字为"蓟"。公元前1045年北京成为蓟、燕等诸侯国的都城；公元前221年秦始皇统一中国以来，北京一直是中国北方重镇和地方中心；自公元938年以来，北京又先后成为辽陪都、金上都、元大都、明清国都。1949年10月1日正式定为中华人民共和国首都。

旅游资源

北京具有丰富的旅游资源，对外开放的旅游景点达200多处，有世界上最大的皇宫紫禁城、祭天神庙天坛、皇家花园北海、皇家园林颐和园，还有八达岭、慕田峪、司马

台长城及世界上最大的四合院恭王府等名胜古迹。全市共有文物古迹 7,309 项，其中国家级文物保护单位42 个，市级文物保护单位 222 个。北京的市树为国槐和侧柏，市花为月季和菊花。另外，北京出产的象牙雕刻、玉器雕刻、景泰蓝、地毯等传统手工艺品驰誉世界。

3　Numerals 数字听译练习

A 单纯数字听译练习

Country	Area（km^2）	Population
Estonia	45,277	1,340,000
Finland	338,417	5,352,000
France	632,834	6,545,000
Greece	131,957	11,310,000
Hungary	93,030	10,010,000
Iceland	103,000	319,000
Ireland	70,282	4,420,000
Italy	301,333	60,020,000
Luxembourg	2,586.3	493,500
Macedonia	25,713	2,048,000
Malta	316	413,600
Moldova	33,800	3,560,000
Monaco	2	34,021

B 带有数字的句子听译练习

1. A survey finds that 30 percent of students say cheating during tests happens quite often, and over 65 percent admit asking their friends for help even when a professor has told them to work alone.

2. Within a decade of the introduction of the Divorce Law, the total divorce rate rose from 14% of all marriages in 1989 to 30% in 2008.

3. The Chinese currency has appreciated by more than 8% since July, 2005, when the country allowed the Yuan to float against the US dollar within a daily band of 0.3%.

4. This morning, I am going to talk briefly about consumer price changes in five major countries. As you can see, the annual change in consumer prices rose from around 4% in 2002 to just under 6% in 2004 in the US.

5. By the year 2000, the population of the developing world living in urban areas had risen to about 46% and it is estimated to reach more than 57% by the year 2025.

4 Idioms Interpreting 成语练习

A From English to Chinese

1. Gold can't be pure and man can't be perfect.
2. What's lost is lost.
3. The friendship between gentlemen is as pure as crystal.
4. Where there is life, there is hope.
5. When wine is in, truth is out.
6. A bad beginning makes a bad ending.
7. When riches increase, the body decreases.
8. When the cat's away the mice will play.
9. Bread is the staff of life.
10. The highest towers begin from the ground.

B From Chinese to English

1. 只要活着，就有希望。
2. 名利双收。
3. 失去自由即失去一切。
4. 没有规矩不成方圆。
5. 每逢佳节倍思亲。
6. 谋事在人，成事在天。
7. 为善最乐。
8. 巧妇难为无米之炊。
9. 千里之行，始于足下。
10. 前事不忘，后事之师。

5 Linear Interpreting for Sentences 句子顺译练习

A From English to Chinese

1. Here are the details. Your guide will meet you in the hotel lobby at 10 a.m. tomorrow morning. Her name is Wang Ping.
2. Traveling broadens my mind and offers me a chance to make friends with people from different parts of the world.
3. With the improvement of our living standard, more and more people will go traveling on their holidays.
4. It is worth visiting the Three Gorges area, which has the picturesque landscape and rich natural resources.
5. The climate is pleasant; the environment is beautiful; the resource is abundant; the transportation is convenient; the infrastructure is complete. This is really a

treasured land.

B From Chinese to English

1. 丽江和西宁作为全国两座旅游热点城市，有很多引人入胜的人文景观和自然景观。
2. 滨江公园因其特殊的地理位置、优美的环境、一流的管理，博得了市民的青睐，是人们休闲、健身、游玩的首选之地。
3. 我要订 9 月 15 号到纽约的班机。
4. 我可能有一个来自美国的团队，需要你的合作，并需要你确定以下内容。
5. 在英国用谈论天气作引子开始交谈并不罕见。在新加坡听人们用不同的语言交谈并不罕见。

6 Sight Interpreting for Passages 段落视译练习

A From English to Chinese

Of all the notable mountains in China, Mount Huangshan, to be found in the south of Anhui Province, is probably the most famous. Originally known as Mt. Yishan, it was renamed Mt. Huangshan in 747 AD in recognition of the legendary Huang Di, who was the reputed ancestor of the Chinese people and who made magic pills for immortality here.

Wu Yue is the collective name given to China's most important mountains, namely Mt. Taishan in Shandong Province, Mt. Huashan in Shanxi Province, Mt. Hengshan in Shanxi Province, Mt. Songshan in Henan Province and Mt. Hengshan in Hunan Province. It is said that you won't want to visit any other mountains after seeing Wu Yue, but you won't wish to see even Wu Yue after returning from Mt. Huangshan. This saying may give you some idea of the beauty and uniqueness of Mt. Huangshan. Together with the Yellow River, the Yangtze River and the Great Wall, Mt. Huangshan has become one of the great symbols of China.

Mt. Huangshan boasts not only its magnificence but also its abundant resources and a great variety of zoological species, for which it has been listed as a World Natural and Cultural Heritage Site.

B From Chinese to English

长江是中国第一大河，仅次于非洲的尼罗河和南美洲的亚马孙河，为世界第三长河。它全长 6 300 千米，流域面积 180.9 万平方千米。长江中下游地区气候温暖湿润、雨量充沛、土地肥沃，是中国重要的农业区；长江还是中国东西水上运输的大动脉，有"黄金水道"之称。黄河是中国第二大河，全长 5 464 千米，流域面积 75.2 万平方千米。黄河流域牧场丰美、矿藏富饶，历史上曾是中国古代文明的发祥地之一。黑龙江是中国北部的一条大河，全长 4 350 千米，其中有 3 101 千米流经中国境内。珠江为中国南部的一条大河，全长 2 214 千米。除天然河流外，中国还有一条著名的人工河，那就是贯穿南北的大运河。它始凿于公元前 5 世纪，北起北京，南到浙江杭州，沟通海河、黄河、淮河、长江、钱塘江五大水系，全长 1 801 千米，是世界上开凿最早、最长的人工河。

Unit 5

Shopping & Dining
购物美食

 I. Objectives

After reading this unit, you are required to

☑ practice memory and note-taking techniques.

☑ get familiar with expressions related to shopping and dining.

☑ find ways to improve your social etiquettes at table.

II. Vocabulary Work

---

1. counter	*n.* 柜台	21. cafeteria	*n.* 自助餐厅
2. stall/stand	*n.* 售货摊	22. napkin	*n.* 餐巾
3. shelf	*n.* 货架	23. entree	*n.* 正菜
4. discount	*n.* 折扣	24. dessert	*n.* 甜食
5. change	*n.* 零钱	25. appetizer	*n.* 开胃菜
6. salesman/saleswoman	*n.* 售货员	26. snack	*n.* 点心，小吃
7. cosmetics	*n.* 化妆用品	27. pudding	*n.* 布丁
8. stationery	*n.* 文具	28. dim sum	*n.* 点心
9. fabrics	*n.* 纺织品	29. saucer	*n.* 小碟
10. towel	*n.* 毛巾	30. teapot	*n.* 茶壶
11. handkerchief	*n.* 手帕	31. coffeepot	*n.* 咖啡壶
12. shampoo	*n.* 洗发香波	32. tray	*n.* 托盘
13. soap	*n.* 肥皂	33. toothpick	*n.* 牙签
14. detergent	*n.* 洗衣粉	34. picnic	*n.* （郊游）野餐
15. lipstick	*n.* 口红，唇膏	35. banquet	*n.* 宴会
16. perfume	*n.* 香水	36. feast	*n.* 盛宴
17. needle	*n.* 针	37. buffet	*n.* 自助餐
18. button	*n.* 纽扣	38. specialty	*n.* 招牌菜
19. zipper	*n.* 拉链	39. vegetarianism	*n.* 素食主义
20. bargain	*n./v.* 讨价还价	40. seafood	*n.* 海鲜

III. Phrase Interpreting

A **From English to Chinese**

1. shopping centre
2. department store
3. antique shop
4. second-hand store
5. show/shop window
6. installment payment
7. cashier's desk
8. price tag
9. out of stock
10. free of charge

B **From Chinese to English**

1. 老字号
2. 摆桌子
3. 餐桌礼仪
4. 水果盘
5. 烤牛排
6. 橘子汁
7. 喝醉
8. 茶道
9. 店内吃或外卖
10. 小笼包

IV. Sentence Interpreting

A **From English to Chinese**

1. Please give me a cream birthday cake and two boxes of famous Chinese cakes.
2. There are many cooking methods for Chinese food, but the most commonly used are frying, stir-frying, braising, stewing and simmering.
3. Chinese culinary art has a long history, and Chinese food is well-known for its color, aroma, taste and shape.
4. Beijing has a well-reserved reputation for roast duck. The best place to have a taste of it is Quanjude Roast Duck Restaurant.
5. This skirt matches this blouse, doesn't it? Could you tell me how much it is?

B **From Chinese to English**

1. 请帮我把这个包起来。我可不可以用信用卡付账?
2. 大型购物中心非常方便,因为我们在那里几乎可以买到所需要的任何东西。
3. 法式菜肴的特点是花样极多,这一点可与中国菜肴或印度菜肴相媲美。
4. 尽管大多数美国人喜欢吃快餐,但他们也特别喜欢在节假日和家人聚在餐桌旁吃大餐。

5. 如果你吃不完，你可以把剩下的菜打包带走。

V. Dialogue Interpreting

Directions：*Interpret the following conversation alternatively into English and Chinese.*

Shopping at an Outlet

Eliza：This place is great. I'm surprised they have so much.

Jane：是啊，但找东西需要一点儿时间就是了。这里不像一般的店那样井然有序。

Eliza：I never shopped in an outlet before. We don't have any in my hometown. Why do they call it an "outlet"?

Jane：有时候成衣公司生产过量，不能在各店销完，只好把存货送到大卖场来，所以叫作"出清"。也就是商家把各店没卖出去的货清出去。

Eliza：And they have faulty products here too.

Jane：是的，"瑕疵品"可能是一件有缺陷的衬衫，或是一条有破洞的裤子。有时候瑕疵很小，所以很值得买的。如果你有针线，可以买回家再做修补。

Eliza：I like to sew, so that's easy for me. I think it's a really good deal. Some of these shirts have only one tiny mistake on them.

Jane：我知道。有时候在大卖场购物是一个好主意，你可以省很多钱。

Eliza：That's great for me. Now that Steve and I have the baby, we want to save as much as we can.

Cashier：太太，付现金还是刷卡？

Eliza：Credit.

Jane：哇，你买多少件汗衫呢？

Eliza：I have six here.

Jane：六件？为什么你需要这么多呢？

Eliza：They're such a good deal. I'm buying one for Steve, one for his brother Rick, one for my dad, two for my sisters, and one for me.

Jane：你真的很会逛大卖场！

Eliza：I ought to make the most of it while I'm here, don't you think?

Jane：当然，你真聪明。

VI. Text Interpreting

Ⓐ **From English to Chinese**

In the United States, fast food is very popular and fast food restaurants are every-

where. Most of the fast food restaurants sell hamburgers, French fries, milk shakes, ice-cream, etc. There are also fast food restaurants that serve Chinese, Italian or Mexican food.

Why is fast food so popular in the US? The most important reason is that the pace of life is so fast in America. People usually have a short lunch break, and they have no time to linger over their meal. Fast food restaurants are very considerate of customer's time. Their fast food is usually ready before it is ordered. You can just order your food and then take it immediately to a table, picking up things like straws, pepper, salt and napkins on the way. You can also order your food "to go" and then take it away and eat it anywhere you like. Some fast food restaurants have driving facilities. It means that you can get served without leaving your car. You place your order from your car via a microphone and then drive round to a special window to pay and pick it up. Another reason is that fast food items are inexpensive and people can afford to eat at a fast food restaurant often.

B **From Chinese to English**

尽管有禽流感的威胁，鸡肉仍然是当今最受欢迎的肉食品，这有几个原因。第一，鸡肉价格合理，人人皆可接受。第二，鸡肉吃法众多，比如，可以同通心粉汁或面条或汤一起煮。鸡肉可以烧、煮或炸着吃。最后也是最重要的一个原因是，鸡肉营养价值很高。4 盎司的鸡肉含有 28 克的蛋白质，那几乎是推荐人体每日摄入量的一半了。

VII. Enhancement Practice

 1 Shadow-speaking in English 英语影子练习

Directions：*Listen to the MP3 and reiterate what you have heard simultaneously*

Talking about Haggling

（Mike and Amanda are talking about haggling.）

Mike： Hi, Amanda, what do you think of my new sneakers? I just bought them at Wu Fang Pu a few days ago. They look pretty nice.

Amanda： Mike. I especially like that color. What a striking shade of blue! How much did you end up paying for them?

Mike： Well, after a bit of haggling, I was able to convince the salesperson to sell them to me for 730 NT dollars. The original price was 750 NT dollars. So I think I got myself a pretty sweet deal.

Amanda: 730 NT dollars is in bet. But I don't think you should be patting yourself on the back for your bargaining skills. You only saved 20 NT dollars. Why didn't you try to get a better price than that?

Mike: I did, but then the girl of the store told me that she wouldn't make any profit if she gave me the sneakers for cheaper. She said if she lowered the price any more, her boss would just deduct the money directly from her paycheck or maybe even fire her.

Amanda: Oh, Mike, Don't you know that's what they always say when you are trying to haggle. You have to be merciless. You can't let your emotions cloud your judgment and you have to walk away.

Mike: I should bring you along the next time I go shopping.

2 Memory & Note-taking 记忆、笔记练习

A English Passage Retelling

Directions: *This part is to test your short-term memory and note-taking skills. You are required to repeat what you have heard from the recording. You may take notes while you're listening. This passage will be played only once.*

Hainan Island, the second largest island in China, lies in the far south, with an area of over 32,200 square kilometers. It faces the Leizhou Peninsula across the Qiongzhou Strait to the north.

Hainan is high in the middle and low on all sides. Five-Finger Mountain is the most famous mountain on the island. Seen from the southeast, the main peak is like five fingers.

One will enjoy tropical scenery everywhere on Hainan. There is a large area of tropical forest, a variety of evergreen plants, plus many special biological phenomena, such as plate-like roots, blossoms on old stems and so on.

Hainan is the main production area for tropical cash crops such as rubber, coconuts, oil palms, and pepper, etc.

It is a famous tourist place, reputed to be a "pearl" in the South China Sea. Moreover, Sanya City in the south has green seawater, blue sky and charming scenery. Many famous scenic spots such as Tooth Dragon Bay, Great East Sea, End of the Earth and Deer Looking Back, attract thousands of visitors every day.

B Chinese Passage Retelling

Directions: *This part is to test your short-term memory and note-taking skills. You are required to repeat what you have heard from the recording. You may take notes* *while you're listening. This passage will be played only once.*

粤菜是我国四大菜系之一，粤菜即广东地方风味菜，主要由广州、潮州、东江三种风味组成，以广州风味为代表。粤菜具有独特的南国风味，并以选料广博、菜肴新颖奇异而著称于世。

粤菜，有广州菜、潮州菜和东江菜三大类。粤菜集南海、番禺、东莞、顺德、中山等地方风味的特色，兼京、苏、扬、杭等外省菜及西菜之所长，融为一体，自成一家。粤菜取百家之长，用料广博，选料珍奇，配料精巧，善于在模仿中创新，依食客喜好而烹制。味重清、鲜、爽、滑、嫩、脆，讲求镬气，调味遍及"酸甜苦辣咸鲜"，菜肴有"香酥脆肥浓"之别，"五滋六味"俱全。如京都骨、炸熘黄鱼、虾爆鳝背等，吸取京菜口味创制；铁板牛肉、鱼香鸡球、宫保鸡丁等，借鉴川菜口味；五柳鱼、东坡肉、酒呛虾是浙菜口味；闻名岭南的太爷鸡是徽菜口味；而西汁猪扒、茄汁牛排等，则是从西菜移植而来。

粤菜选料广博奇异，品种花样繁多，令人眼花缭乱。天上飞的，地上爬的，水中游的，几乎都能上席。

粤菜的另一突出特点是，用量精而细，配料多而巧，装饰美而艳，而且善于在模仿中创新，品种繁多，1965 年"广州名菜美点展览会"介绍的就有 5 457 种之多。

粤菜的第三个特点是，注重质和味，口味比较清淡，力求清中求鲜、淡中求美。而且，粤菜随季节时令的变化而变化，夏秋偏重清淡，冬春偏重浓郁，追求色、香、味、型。粤菜食味讲究清、鲜、嫩、爽、滑、香，调味遍及酸、甜、苦、辣、咸，此即所谓五滋六味。

3　Numerals 数字听译练习

Ⓐ 单纯数字听译练习

The World's Top Ten Banks

Bank	Primary Capital	Total Assets	Profits
1. Citigroup	41, 889, 000	668, 641, 000	9, 269, 000
2. Bank of America Corp.	36, 877, 000	617, 679, 000	8, 048, 000
3. HSBC Holdings	29, 352, 000	484, 655, 000	6, 591, 000
4. Credit Agricole	25, 930, 000	457, 037, 000	3, 765, 000
5. Chase Manhattan Corp.	24, 121, 000	365, 875, 000	5, 980, 000
6. Industrial&Commercial Bank of China	22, 213, 000	391, 213, 000	417, 000
7. Bank of Tokyo-Mitsubishi	22, 074, 000	598, 720, 000	156, 000
8. Union Bank of Switzerland	20, 525, 000	685, 882, 000	2, 957, 000
9. Sakura Bank	19, 899, 000	389, 434, 000	5, 866, 000
10. Bank One Corp.	19, 654, 000	261, 496, 000	4, 465, 000

带有数字的句子听译练习

1. In the first three quarters of 2008, the annual fiscal income of the province increased by 350 billion yuan.

2. The four-star tourist garden hotel has 97 deluxe suites, 268 standard rooms, and a convention hall with a seating capacity of over 450 people.

3. In recent years, Shanghai has pumped some 10 percent of its GNP and 40 percent of its total fixed assets investment into the construction of the city's infrastructure.

4. Australia is one of the most urbanized countries in the world, with about 70 percent of the population living in the 10 largest cities.

5. January 26, the date of the first European settlement of the continent in 1788, is Australia's National Day.

4 Idioms Interpreting 习语口译练习

A From English to Chinese

1. Kill two birds with one stone.
2. Until all is over one's ambition never dies.
3. Fine feathers make fine birds.
4. Beat the dog before the lion.
5. Teach fish to swim.
6. Peace on the forehead and war in the mind.
7. Rest breeds rust.
8. A watched pot never boils.
9. Let sleeping dogs lie.
10. Save your breath to cool your porridge.

B From Chinese to English

1. 开卷有益。
2. 寸金难买寸光阴。
3. 无事不登三宝殿。
4. 教学相长。
5. 以其人之道，还治其人之身。
6. 骄者必败。
7. 名师出高徒。
8. 公事公办。
9. 历史总在重演。
10. 欲速则不达。

5 Linear Interpreting for Sentences 句子顺译练习

A From English to Chinese

1. Make yourself at home and help yourself to the dishes.
2. Would you like to try my special recipe?
3. Maotai is China's best-known liquor; it is delicious and yet doesn't go to the head.

4. Fast-food restaurants can be seen all over the country. Speed is a very important factor in the life of an American.

5. Traditionally, everyone at the Chinese dining table has his or her own bowl of staple food, that is, steamed rice, noodles or steamed bread, while the dishes are placed in the middle of the dinner table to be shared by all.

B From Chinese to English

1. 这个购物中心早上九点开门，晚上九点半关门。节假日和周末人多极了。

2. 这件颜色太鲜艳了，请给我拿一件暗一点儿的。

3. 这是个千载难逢的机会。价格已经很合理了，几乎是成本价。

4. 如果鞋子不合适您，您可以凭收据七天内换货。

5. 对不起，我们没有这种现货，也许您可以去我们的前门分店碰碰运气。

6 Sight Interpreting for Passages 段落视译练习

A From English to Chinese

In most cultures, meals may have certain form that makes people know what to expect. When the English see tea, or when Americans see coffee, they know dinner is over.

While American Chinese food may have been adapted to American tastes, it has not been adapted to American form. Americans who are accustomed to a main course topped off by a big dessert often do not know when the Chinese meal is over.

Generally speaking, dinners are much less formal and elaborate in the United States than in China. In China, the number of different dishes served at each meal is really impressive. It is impossible to finish everything.

In the United States, when guests come to a home for dinner, the host or hostess usually serves one main dish, and one dessert. Guests may very likely consume all that is offered.

B From Chinese to English

圣 诞 讲 话

谢谢各位！

此时此刻，我们在此共度祖国首都的一个重要的传统节日。整个圣诞节我们感到上帝之爱遍洒人间每个角落，人人都享有上帝恩赐的和平。能在这和平的圣诞晚会与大家相聚，我和我夫人无比高兴。为此我也要感谢诸位的光临。

感谢戈尔先生主持这个晚会。感谢所有的演艺人员，感谢你们使这个夜晚如此特别，谢谢你们的到来。感谢董事会和所有的筹备人员，是你们组织了这场精彩的盛事。感谢圣诞老人的光临。最后，我要感谢这里所有辛勤工作的人们。

近 80 年来，不论是在安定的生活中还是在遇到挑战的时候，美国人都要为这个节日欢聚一堂。关于这个节日的圣诞故事我们都知道，它感召着一代又一代人。两千多年来，圣诞节一直传递着一个信息——上帝与我们同在。正是因为他与我们同在，我们才能永远生活在希望之中。

现在，我们与家人同庆如此良辰佳节，并深切缅怀那些离我们而去的亲人。我们国家有千万家庭仍在为去年 9 月 11 日他们所蒙受的巨大损失而哀恸。我们祈祷他们安心，我们祈祷所有今年失败、沮丧的人安心。

我和我夫人祝愿所有的美国家庭节日好运、假期愉快、圣诞快乐！现在，我们非常荣幸地来点亮这棵国家圣诞树。如果你们都已准备好，请走上前来。请大家和我们一起倒计时：五、四、三、二、一。

Unit **6**

Fashion & Sports
时尚运动

I. Objectives

After reading this unit, you are required to

☑ practice memory and note-taking techniques.

☑ get familiar with expressions related to fashion and sports.

☑ master the basic skills of sight interpretation.

II. Vocabulary Work

1. fashion　*n.*　时尚	16. champion　*n.*　冠军
2. blog　*n.*　博客，网络日记	17. athlete　*n.*　运动员
3. dynamic　*n.*　动感	18. instructor/coach　*n.*　教练，技术指导
4. cool　*a.*　酷	19. referee　*n.*　裁判
5. winger　*n.*　新潮人物	20. professional　*n./a.*　职业运动员（的）
6. alternative　*n.*　另类	21. amateur　*n./a.*　业余运动员，爱好者；业余的
7. speculation　*n.*　炒作	22. sportsmanship　*n.*　体育道德
8. netizen　*n.*　网民	23. stadium/gymnasium　*n.*　运动场
9. hacker　*n.*　黑客	24. track　*n.*　跑道
10. virus　*n.*　病毒	25. gymnastics　*n.*　体操
11. inflation　*n.*　通货膨胀	26. weight-lifting　*n.*　举重
12. cyberlove　*n.*　网恋	27. boxing　*n.*　拳击
13. fan　*n.*　粉丝，迷	28. skiing　*n.*　滑雪
14. idol　*n.*　偶像	29. rugby　*n.*　橄榄球
15. bungee　*n.*　蹦极	30. badminton　*n.*　羽毛球

III. Phrase Interpreting

A From English to Chinese

1. Olympic Games

2. International Olympic Committee

3. international tournament

4. competition gymnasiums and stadiums

5. competitive sport

6. physical culture and sports

7. track and field

8. organizing committee

9. sporting/sports power 10. produce an unexpected winner

B From Chinese to English

1. 追星族 2. 写真集
3. 单身贵族 4. 丁克族
5. 新新人类 6. 人体彩绘
7. 考研热 8. 反恐
9. AA 制 10. 春运

 # IV. Sentence Interpreting

A From English to Chinese

1. Many experts point out that physical exercise contributes directly to a person's physical fitness.
2. Furthermore, people who addict to fashion clothes have to spend more time going shopping and pay more attention to the impression they make on others. As a result, it is impossible to devote enough time and energy to their study and job.
3. However, this idea is now being questioned by more and more experts, who point out that it is unhealthy for children who always stay with their parents at home.
4. Many people seem to overlook the basic fact: the major function of clothing is to keep us warm and comfortable.
5. It is suggested that governments ought to make efforts to reduce the increasing gap between cities and countryside. They ought to set aside an appropriate fund for the improvement of the standard of farmers' lives.

B From Chinese to English

1. 近些年，关于时尚存在着广泛的争论。其中一个问题就是一个人是否应选择他喜欢的舒适的衣服，而不管是否时尚。
2. 中国的社区体育开展得如何？很好！社区体育十分繁荣，经常有各种业余比赛。
3. 农民进城打工正呈现增长的趋势，这一问题在世界上大部分城市已引起普遍关注。
4. 奥林匹克的标志是五个相连的圆环，它代表着五大洲的团结和全世界运动员在奥运会上相聚一堂。
5. 健美操是我最喜欢的运动。这对腰部的瘦身十分有效。你不认为我的腰围变得越来越小了吗？

V. Dialogue Interpreting

Directions：*Interpret the following conversation alternatively into English and Chinese.*

（P = Peter　T = Ted）

P ： 啊，天气真好。到户外活动活动怎么样？

T ： OK. The air is so fresh.

P ： 平常你喜欢什么样的活动？

T ： I'm fond of the shuttle cock, the seesaw and playing basketball.　How about you?

P ： 我喜欢跳舞、游泳等。

T ： Which one do you like best?

P ： 我认为什么运动都不如游泳。

T ： Why?

P ： 因为它能增强我们全身的机能。

T ： How many strokes are there usually?

P ： 有自由泳、仰泳、蝶泳、蛙泳等。

T ： I heard exercise can also boost brain function.

P ： 是的，锻炼能促进血液流动和细胞生成，而且运动还能减肥。

T ： A growing keep-fit fever is sweeping over China, isn't it?

P ： 为了过上幸福的生活，谁不想有个健康的身体，谁不想长寿啊。

T ： What do they play with usually?

T ： 对退休年龄的人，他一般打打太极拳、舞舞剑、练练中国武术。

T ： How about young people?

P ： 现在许多年轻人都时兴到健身房锻炼。

VI. Text Interpreting

 English Passage Retelling

Football

Making the soccer sector professional has raised the level of the Chinese team. The Chinese national team's desire to compete in the World Cup finals has been frustrated too many times. For a long time, people in the soccer circle and those concerned about Chinese soccer explored ways to improve the game. In 1994, professionalized leagues began to be practiced in China.

It brought changes to Chinese soccer. A great improvement in the player's skills, ideas and concepts was seen. Another change brought about by the professionalized league is the involvement of foreign athletes. Nowadays, soccer is no longer a game merely for entertainment, but also a carrier of modern culture, economy and social activities. The World Cup has become a tool to measure the soccer level of a country.

B **Chinese Passage Retelling**

爱情是一种感觉，婚姻是一个约定，而夫妻关系则是一门功课。

这对于上海很多婚姻不幸福的年轻夫妇们来说的确是个现实。他们面临的选择是，要么努力解决好两人之间的问题，要么离婚。

而现在看来，很多人还是选择了放弃。

据官方统计数据，很多30岁以下的夫妇（大多是80年后的独生子女）选择的是离婚，而不是和解。

最新数据显示，从今年1月至5月，上海有2 100对年轻夫妇离婚，比2006年上升10%。

去年，上海平均每天有102对夫妻离婚。其中，80年后出生的、年龄不到30岁的夫妇离婚率最高，去年上海共有5 876对30岁以下的夫妇离婚。

一家离婚服务公司的创建者舒心说，80年后的人比其他年龄段的人更有"离婚倾向"，他们更需要婚姻咨询服务。

舒女士说："与上几代的人相比，80年后的一代以自我为中心的意识更强。"

"所以在婚姻中遇到问题时，很多人就会用草率离婚的方式来逃避问题。"

华东理工大学的张雄副教授说，年轻夫妇"做离婚决定过于草率"，这是离婚率逐年上升的一个重要因素。

 # VII. Enhancement Practice

1 Shadow-speaking in English 英语影子练习

Directions: *Listen to the MP3 and reiterate what you have heard simultaneously.*

Today, with the development of the market economy in China, designs or styles of fashions are so dazzling as the stars that the eye cannot take them all in. As a result, people are often at a loss what to choose when facing the vast sea of fashions. On the other hand, it is just a golden opportunity for Chinese national costumes to regain their popularity. Fashion culture has become a point of intersection of social culture, reflecting economic developments, social progress and educational level.

Qipao, the classic dress for Chinese women, combines the elaborate elegance of Chinese tradition with unique elements of style. The high-necked, closed-collar Qipao, with a loose chest, fitting waist, and the attractive slits, is one of the most versatile costumes in the world. It can be long or short, some with full, medium, short or even no sleeves at all — to suit different occasions, weather and individual tastes.

The Qipao can display all women's modesty, softness and beauty. Like Chinese women's temperament, the Qipao is elegant and gentle, its long-standing elegance and serenity makes wearers fascinating. Mature women in Qipao can display their graceful refined manner. A Qipao almost varies with a woman's figure.

2 Memory & Note-taking 记忆、笔记练习

A English Passage Retelling

Directions： *This part is to test your short-term memory and note-taking skills. You are required to repeat what you have heard from the recording. You may take notes while you're listening. This passage will be played only once.*

For China, this has been a special year. We experienced two major events. One was the devastating earthquake in Wenchuan, which cause grave losses of life and property. In the face of the disaster, the Chinese people showed great strength, courage, solidarity and resilience. By now, the people affected by the earthquake have been properly relocated and recovery and reconstruction work is well underway. The other was the successful hosting of the Beijing Olympic Games. This grand sporting event provided a good opportunity for athletes from around the world to show true sportsmanship. It also enabled the world to learn more about China and China more about the world. In our fight against the earthquake disaster and our efforts to host the Games, we received understanding, support and assistance from the international community. I wish to take this opportunity to express sincere gratitude on behalf of the Chinese Government and people.

B Chinese Passage Retelling

Directions： *This part is to test your short-term memory and note-taking skills. You are required to repeat what you have heard from the recording. You may take notes while you're listening. This passage will be played only once.*

罗格宣布北京奥运会闭幕　称其"真正的无与伦比"

中新网 8 月 24 日电　第 29 届奥林匹克运动会闭幕式今晚在中国国家体育场"鸟巢"举行，国际奥委会主席罗格在致辞中宣布第 29 届奥林匹克运动会闭幕，并称本届奥运会是一届真正的无与伦比的奥运会。

罗格致辞全文如下：

亲爱的中国朋友们，今晚，我们即将走到 16 天光辉历程的终点。这些日子，将在我们的心中永远珍藏，感谢中国人民，感谢所有出色的志愿者，感谢北京奥组委。

通过本届奥运会，世界更多地了解了中国，中国更多地了解了世界，来自 204 个国家和地区奥委会的运动健儿们在光彩夺目的场馆里同场竞技，用他们的精湛技艺博得了我们的赞叹。

新的奥运明星诞生了，往日的奥运明星又一次带来惊喜，我们分享他们的欢笑和泪水，我们钦佩他们的才能与风采，我们将长久铭记再次见证的辉煌成就。

在庆祝奥运会圆满成功之际，让我们一起祝福才华横溢的残奥会运动健儿们，希望他们在即将到来的残奥会上取得优秀的成绩。他们也令我们倍感鼓舞，今晚在场的每位运动员们，你们是真正的楷模，你们充分展示了体育的凝聚力。

来自冲突国家竞技对手的热情拥抱之中闪耀着奥林匹克精神的光辉。希望你们回国后让这种精神生生不息，世代永存。

这是一届真正的无与伦比的奥运会，现在，遵照惯例，我宣布第 29 届奥林匹克运动会闭幕，并号召全世界青年四年后在伦敦举办的第 30 届奥林匹克运动会上相聚。

谢谢大家！

3 Numerals 数字听译练习

A 单纯数字听译练习

世界 1 000 家银行中我国 7 家银行实力排名表

Rank	Bank	Primary Capital	Total Assets	Profits
6	Industrial & Commercial Bank of China	22, 213, 000	391, 213, 000	417, 000
18	Bank of China	14, 712, 000	299, 007, 000	425, 000
65	Construction Bank of China	5, 988, 000	203, 116, 000	1, 215, 000
99	Agricultural Bank of China	4, 802, 000	190, 095, 000	95, 000
129	Bank of Communications	2, 816, 000	58, 454, 000	322, 000
300	Merchants Bank	974, 000	16, 679, 000	242, 000
938	Xiamen International Bank	163, 000	1, 208, 000	22, 000

B 带有数字的句子听译练习

1. So far, more than 400, 000 people have sent in applications, more than 270, 000 of them from Beijing.

2. According to a recent survey, four million people die each year from diseases linked to smoking.

3. We face the worst economic crisis since the Great Depression — 760, 000 workers

have lost their jobs this year. Wages are lower than they've been in a decade, at a time when the costs of health care and college have never been higher.

4. A solar heating system comprising nearly 6,000 square meters of solar panels will provide hot water for bathrooms in the Olympics Village, where 16,800 athletes from various countries will be staying. After the Olympics, this system will continue to supply hot water to more than 2,000 households in the area.

5. The American economy decreased between July and September more than first thought. A government report says a measure of all the goods and services produced in the United States shrank by 0.5% during the period. That is 0.2% worse than first estimated.

4 Idioms Interpreting 习语口译练习

A From English to Chinese

1. Give me liberty, or give me death!
2. Old horse knows the way.
3. Good wine needs no bush.
4. love at first sight
5. The pupil outdoes the master.
6. There are plenty of fish in the sea.
7. Diamond cut diamond.
8. He takes a spear to kill a fly.
9. Gifts blind the eyes.
10. Dogs bite in every country.

B From Chinese to English

1. 英雄所见略同。
2. 祸不单行。
3. 学而时习之，不亦说乎？
4. 学以致用。
5. 温故而知新。
6. 岁月不饶人。
7. 少小不努力，老大徒伤悲。
8. 健康胜过财富。
9. 无官一身轻。
10. 居安思危。

5 Linear Interpreting for Sentences 句子顺译练习

A From English to Chinese

1. All employees of various agencies working in the non-government or service unit sectors, and employees of state-owned enterprises are excluded from the civil service.

2. Generally speaking, Americans express themselves openly and freely. It's not considered good to beat around the bush.

3. I think some people regard handicrafts as something mysterious and troublesome,

but to me, it's great pleasure.

4. China is a multi-ethnic country where minority nationalities make up about 6% of the total population. They are concentrated in strategically important border areas such as Tibet, Xinjiang, Yunnan, and Inner Mongolia, but also make up substantial portions of the populations of Guizhou, Sichuan, Ningxia, Hubei, and Hunan provinces.

5. The beauty of a woman is not in the clothes she wears, the figure that she carries, or the way she combs her hair. The beauty of a woman must be seen from in her eyes, because that is the doorway to her heart, the place where love resides.

B From Chinese to English

1. 中国人普遍称呼姓氏和头衔；对人表示尊重很重要；与人保持一定距离被认为是有礼貌的表现。

2. 在我们这里当公务员必须有计算机。我们要充分利用信息高速公路的发展成果。

3. 女人的美丽不在于外表，真正的美丽折射于一个女人的灵魂深处，在于亲切的给予和热情。

4. 在日本，个人空间相对较小，25 厘米左右。但是在美国，个人空间就大得多，45 厘米左右。

5. 国家体育场，又被称作鸟巢，是北京 2008 年奥运会的主会场，在这里将举行奥运会的开幕式、闭幕式，以及全部的田径比赛，可以容纳观众 10 万人。

6 Sight Interpreting for Passages 段落视译练习

A From English to Chinese

Move over Michael Phelps, the Beijing Olympics has another superstar.

Usain Bolt blazed into the Olympic history books last night, becoming the first man to break world records while winning both 100m and 200 m races at a single Games.

The Jamaican broke the world record by winning the 200m in 19. 30 second, becoming also the first man since American Carl Lewis in 1984 to sweep the 100 m and 200 m gold medals at an Olympics.

Bolt, who turns 22 today, took the top spot on the heels of his win in the men's 100 m on Saturday.

He bettered his own world record in that race by winning in 9. 69 second, despite slowing down over the final 20 m to showboat.

"I am No. 1. I am No. 1!" the world's fastest man declared to TV audiences as he beat his chest and blew kisses at the 91,000 crowd in the Bird's Nest, before continuing with his victory lap.

B **From Chinese to English**

奥 运 之 路

　　20 世纪初，成为奥林匹克大家庭的一员仍只是中国人的一个梦想。1949 年以前，中国运动员曾参加过三届奥运会，均无功而返。1949 年以来，中国政府派代表团先后参加了六届夏季奥运会、七届冬奥会，总计获夏季奥运会金牌 112 枚。其中在洛杉矶、巴塞罗那、亚特兰大奥运会上获金牌总数列第四位；在雅典奥运会上获金牌总数列第二位。

　　1979 年，中国恢复了在国际奥委会的合法席位。1981 年，何振梁当选为国际奥委会委员，中国与奥林匹克运动的关系及与国际奥委会的合作进入了新的历史时期。此后，中国体育界开始积极支持奥林匹克的普及与推动工作，其中重要的一部分是：遵照奥林匹克运动的广泛性原则，使占世界人口五分之一的中国人能够分享举办奥运会的荣誉和欢乐。2001 年 7 月，北京这个有着 3,000 年悠久历史的古都终于获得成功，得到了 2008 年奥运会的主办权。

　　成立于 2001 年底的北京奥组委称"绿色奥运、科技奥运、人文奥运"是 2008 年奥运会的理念。在制定并向社会公布北京奥运会规划后，顺利完成国际招、投标工作的 30 个奥运会场馆自 2003 年起陆续动工兴建。包括国家体育场、国家游泳中心在内的七个场馆的设计构思精妙，被认为将会把北京带入一个新的诗意建筑时代。国家体育场，又被称作鸟巢，是北京 2008 年奥运会的主会场，在这里将举行奥运会的开幕式、闭幕式，以及全部的田径比赛，可以容纳观众 10 万人。

Unit 7 Leisure & Entertainment 休闲娱乐

I. Objectives

After reading this unit, you are required to

☑ practice short-term memory and listening translation techniques.

☑ get familiar with expressions related to fashion and sports.

☑ master basic skills of sight interpretation.

II. Vocabulary Work

1. witty-skits　*n.*　小品
2. Wushu（Chinese Martial Arts）　*n.*　武术
3. cross-talk　*n.*　相声
4. club　*n.*　俱乐部
5. nightclub　*n.*　夜总会
6. carnival　*n.*　狂欢节
7. fireworks　*n.*　焰火
8. picnic　*n.*　野炊
9. swing　*n./v.*　秋千，荡秋千
10. ballet　*n.*　芭蕾舞
11. circus　*n.*　马戏
12. acrobatics　*n.*　杂技
13. conductor　*n.*　（乐队、合唱团的）指挥
14. playwright　*n.*　编剧，剧作家
15. director　*n.*　导演
16. spotlight　*n.*　聚光灯
17. rhythm　*n.*　节奏
18. solo　*n.*　独奏，独唱
19. chorus　*n.*　合唱
20. symphony　*n.*　交响乐
21. opera　*n.*　歌剧
22. comedy　*n.*　喜剧
23. tragedy　*n.*　悲剧
24. melody　*n.*　曲调，旋律
25. rehearsal　*n.*　排演，彩排
26. plot　*n.*　情节
27. climax　*n.*　高潮
28. script　*n.*　剧本
29. interview　*n./v.*　采访
30. fancier/zealot　*n.*　发烧友

III. Phrase Interpreting

A **From English to Chinese**

1. pay New Year calls or visits
2. surf the Internet
3. top notch/big shot
4. disco dancing
5. roller coaster
6. dog packs/paparazzi
7. three-dimensional animation
8. fashion follower

9. variety show 10. puppet show

B From Chinese to English

1. 粉领族 2. 光盘杂志
3. 好莱坞大片 4. 黄金时段
5. 美食节 6. 票房
7. 三维电影 8. 上网
9. 新秀 10. 直播

IV. Sentence Interpreting

A From English to Chinese

1. I'm thinking about going to KTV with my coworkers tonight. Do you like to join us?

2. I'd like to thank you for your presence at the party, and wish everyone good health and the very best of luck in everything in the New Year.

3. Do you have any special plans for the weekend? Maybe we can go hiking. How does that sound?

4. I hope this party will give us an opportunity to get to know each other better in a less formal way and to increase personal friendships.

5. Having enough free time is more important to most Americans than being rich, according to a new poll.

B From Chinese to English

1. 明天晚上咱们不妨举行街坊聚会什么的，好好庆祝一番。我想这个庆祝会倒是值得开的。

2. 人们希望建立更多的医院、购物中心、娱乐中心、电影院和其他公用设施来满足人们日益增长的需求。

3. 事实上，我更喜欢平静的乡村生活而不是现代化的都市生活。

4. 这项表演看上去十分有趣，整群人都被吸引住了。

5. 给家人做饭不仅有趣，而且也是一种表达爱心的方式。

V. Dialogue Interpreting

Directions： *Interpret the following conversation alternatively into English and Chinese.*

史蒂文： 这个周末我们应该带同事们去庆祝一下。

Albert： Yes, the project was a big success. Now that it's finished, I think we should have a party.

史蒂文： 但我不知道要怎么庆祝。我们可以邀请他们去红龙虾餐馆聚餐，然后再来这里喝东西。

Albert： This place?

史蒂文： 对啊，不好吗？这是附近最好的酒吧之一。很多职员住在这儿附近，所以很方便。

Albert： I have a suggestion. Why don't we go to a KTV and sing?

史蒂文： KTV？你说的是真的吗？

Albert： Yes, why not? Don't you like KTVs?

史蒂文： 我不知道，我没去过。

Albert： Never? Really? I'm surprised.

史蒂文： 有什么好惊讶的？很多美国人都没去过 KTV，这不是美国人的活动。

Albert： But there are a lot of KTVs in town. There's one just two blocks from here.

史蒂文： 那是因为这里有很多亚洲移民。他们的客人都是亚洲人。美国人通常不会和朋友出去唱歌。

Albert： I suppose. It's true that when I go to a KTV here in town, there are almost no Westerners.

史蒂文： 你看是吧？

Albert： But you know, Steven — half of the employees in our company are from Japan. So going to a KTV would be fun for them.

史蒂文： 但是其他的职员呢？

Albert： Well, I think you would have a good time too. We'd have to teach you, of course.

VI. Text Interpreting

A From English to Chinese

At the Christmas Party

Mr. Chairman, Ladies and gentlemen,

Merry Christmas to you all!

On behalf of all the members of my group, I'd like to thank you, Mr. Chairman, for your gracious invitation for us to attend such an enjoyable Christmas party in such a magnificently decorated hall.

Christmas is a very happy and joyous occasion. It is really a wonderful time of the year. There is something in this holiday which appeals to everyone. That is, warmth, love, care, union, harmony and dedication of mankind. This is the spirit of the Christmas holiday.

Of course, we really enjoy the delicious wine and excellent food served here. Yes, the roast turkey is simply delicious. Also, the music is superb. If I were a better dancer, I could have enjoyed the party more. I like everything here, but more important, I enjoyed meeting and talking to you, getting to know you, and sharing the memorable time together.

I am deeply grateful for this nice arrangement. The party was perfectly organized and I enjoyed every minute of it. I'm sure I will remember this great occasion for many years to come.

It has been a great year for all of us in terms of our harmonious business relationship. Our joint venture has had a remarkable sales growth. I hope we will be able to maintain this practical cooperative relationship and make the coming new year a more fruitful year.

I would like to toast with you to this happy occasion at the end of the year.

Thank you very much again for this wonderful party. We had a great evening.

Merry Christmas once again to all of you!

B **From Chinese to English**

新 春 联 欢

各位嘉宾：

在这个美丽无比、明月当空的夜晚，我谨代表总经理梅婷女士及公司的全体同仁，感谢各位从百忙中拨冗光临我们的新春联欢晚会。

特别有幸的是，今晚我们请到了从加拿大远道而来的本森电子公司的朋友们。有如此杰出的贵宾与我们一起共同欢度春节，我深感自豪与荣幸。

我们尽自己之所能，并将继续竭尽全力使各位度过一个最轻松、最欢乐、最难忘的夜晚。我希望各位来宾能尽情品尝中国的传统佳肴与美酒。请不要客气。

各位还将欣赏由本公司一些才华横溢的青年员工所表演的纯正中国味的文艺节目。今晚我们会过得非常愉快。平日在公司上班时，我们中外职员几乎没有时间坐下来交谈。我希望这次晚会可以让我们有极好的机会，可以无所拘束地了解彼此的情况，增进个人之间的友谊。

女士们，先生们，我再次感谢各位嘉宾的光临。最后，我祝愿各位新年身体健康、万事如意。

VII. Enhancement Practice

1　Shadow-speaking in English 英语影子练习

Directions：*Listen to the MP3 and reiterate what you have heard simultaneously.*

Talking about Amusement Parks

Mike：Hi, Amanda, happy Friday! Would you have a plan on weekend?

Amanda：Oh, a bunch of my friends and I are going to check out a new amusement park just opened up. Want comes?

Mike：Sure, that sounds like fun. I love an amusement park. What're some of your favorite rides?

Amanda：I always like roller coasters, especially the one goes upside down. The more loops, the better.

Mike：Yeah. Roller coasters can be pretty exaggerating, especially you punch a hundred feet down in five seconds.

Amanda：The only ride I can't stand is the gravity truck.

Mike：Oh, you mean that ride while you're in a big circular room and spin so fast that the first of gravity makes you stick to the walls.

Amanda：Yeah. That ride always makes me nausea. I feel crazy to think about it.

Mike：Tell me about it. When I was eight, I went on that ride after eating. Then after I got a ride, I was so dizzy that I vomited everything I ate all over my shoes.

Amanda：Ah! Mike, I was just about to have lunch.

2　Memory & Note-taking 记忆、笔记练习

A English Passage Retelling

Directions：*This part is to test your short-term memory and note-taking skills. You are required to repeat what you have heard from the recording. You may take notes while you're listening. This passage will be played only once.*

Lao Xu Boasts Soap Opera Life

Xu Jinglei, nicknamed Lao Xu (Old Xu), is the cover girl of *LOHAS* (*Lifestyles of Health and Sustainability*) magazine's December special edition.

Although not so famous outside China, Lao Xu is quite popular domestically as a multi-talented artist. Speaking about her lifestyle during a recent interview with the magazine, Lao Xu said her real life was like a soap opera. She bluntly expressed how painful it would be to live artistically.

Xu rose to fame as an actress. She later became a director, blogger, magazine editor and, most recently, a singer as well. Her Chinese language blog is very popular, having received more than 100 million hits this year.

The article praises Lao Xu for living life by her own rules and seldom caring about what other people may have to say. As she puts it, "You are the only director of your life."

Lao Xu wore a gray sweater from the latest Chanel autumn/winter collection during the interview. However, picky reporters still discovered an outfit clash as Xu was having on her the same styled sweater with the Bond's girl from the latest James Bond movie "Quantum of Solace".

B Chinese Passage Retelling

Directions: *This part is to test your short-term memory and note-taking skills. You are required to repeat what you have heard from the recording. You may take notes while you're listening. This passage will be played only once.*

第 51 届格莱美奖提名公布　英伦摇滚 PK 美国说唱

2008 年 12 月 4 日，洛杉矶，第 51 届格莱美（GRAMMY）音乐奖提名音乐会当地时间 12 月 3 日举行。本次国家录音艺术与科学学会首次采用演唱会的形式宣布格莱美获奖名单，晚会由 CBS 现场直播，节目命名为《格莱美奖提名演唱会直播！——音乐盛典倒计时》（The Grammy Nominations Concert Live! — Countdown to Music's Biggest Night），喷火机（Foo Fighters）、席琳·迪翁（Celine Dion）等大牌歌手都登台献艺为演唱会助兴。之前一直被看好的酷玩乐队（Coldplay）、灵歌小天后达菲及李尔·韦恩都获得了第 51 届格莱美奖的提名。

其中，获得提名最多的美国说唱歌手李尔·韦恩（Lil Wayne）凭借专辑《Tha Carter III》获得 8 项提名。来自英国的酷玩乐队（Coldplay）紧随其后，也得到了 7 项提名。在最受关注的年度专辑大奖提名中，来自美国的两位说唱代表人物李尔·韦恩（Lil Wayne）、Ne-Yo 与来自英国的两支大牌乐队 Coldplay、Radiohead 齐齐入围，鹿死谁手尚数未知，不过现今乐坛依然被英美垄断的局面依然难以撼动。要么英伦摇滚胜出，要么美国说唱大赢，就算年度专辑大奖也由罗伯特·普兰特（Robert Plant）、艾莉森·克劳斯（Alison Krauss）两位老将组合爆冷获得，这支组合也依然是英美混搭（罗伯特·普兰特是英国摇滚乐的先驱，艾莉森·克劳斯则是美国著名的蓝草女歌手）。虽然两大势力超过半个世纪的垄断格局无法轻易改变，起码今年这届格莱美倒有些针锋相对的意思，期待明年 2 月答案揭晓的那一刻。

3 Numerals 数字听译练习

A 单纯数字听译练习

1, 234	4, 567, 809	5, 678, 120, 000	8：00	9：15	11：30
7：50	541 B. C.	1800	1701	2000	in the 1840's
in the 60's	1/3	7/12	1/2	3/4	21/2
20/87	33/90	2. 468	0. 157	20%	16. 09%

B 带有数字的句子听译练习

1. About our appointment for next Tuesday, I wonder whether we could change it from eight to ten.

2. We carry over 30 million passengers a year and we fly to 41 destinations in 25 foreign countries.

3. The traditional pattern of classroom experience at the college level brings the professor and a group of 20 to 30 students together for a 45-to-50-minute class session two or three times a week.

4. The new engine has a capacity of 4. 3 liters and a power out-put of 153 kilowatts at 4, 400 revolutions per minute.

5. The BBC's English teaching radio programs are broadcast daily to four continents and supplied to radio stations in 120 countries. Films and videos are on the air or used in institutions in over 100 countries.

4 Idioms Interpreting 习语口译练习

A From English to Chinese

1. It is such a delight to have friends coming from afar.

2. All are past and gone; we look to this age for truly great men.

3. The way ahead is long; I see no ending, yet high and low I'll search with my will unbending.

4. Learning without thinking leads to confusion; thinking without learning ends in danger.

5. Raising my head, I see the moon so bright; withdrawing my eyes, my nostalgia comes around.

6. Out of sight, out of mind. /Far from eye, far from heart.

7. What you know, you know, what you don't know, you don't know. This is knowledge.

8. Friends must part.

9. The remembrance of the past is the teacher of the future.

10. Many kiss the baby for the nurse's sake.

B **From Chinese to English**

1. 不入虎穴，焉得虎子。   2. 众志成城。

3. 木已成舟。/覆水难收。   4. 真金不怕火炼。

5. 为人不做亏心事，半夜不怕鬼敲门。   6. 天网恢恢，疏而不漏。

7. 万众一心。   8. 灾难有界，大爱无疆。

9. 小巫见大巫。   10. 因小失大。

5 Linear Interpreting for Sentences 句子顺译练习

A **From English to Chinese**

1. I think an actor often plays characters that match his real personality. They are naturally better at such characters.

2. But it was the most disgusting comedy I've ever seen. I think America's values are screwed up if movies like that are popular.

3. I have to agree that's an excellent channel. And maybe, for the first time in history, it's a channel that does some good in the world.

4. I always think it is good to make it to the top, to do one's best. But then, when you've done the best you can, it is good to stop there. In English, we say, "Quit while you're ahead. "

5. I want to go to Monkey Island and look at the monkeys. I love monkeys. That's why I started dating out with you.

B **From Chinese to English**

1. 我是和你一起来旅行的，但是我想你很快就会疲惫不堪，因为你并不是很有经验的滑雪者。所以，可能会花更多的时间在城里逛街购物或在小屋里徘徊吧。

2. 会费一年 15 美元，另外要加收押金 35 美元。当你的会员期限到期时，可以拿回 35 美元。

3. 别浪费钱了，冲浪很困难的，而且今天风很大。他们半小时收费 50 元，你根本冲不起来。你会一直落水的。

4. 我从来就不喜欢玩鬼屋。我小的时候不喜欢，上了中学也不喜欢，上大学时也不喜欢，为什么我现在就会喜欢呢？

5. 尽管大部分人家要等到春节前几个星期才动手准备，可有些中国家庭却这么早就开始准备年货了。

▶ 6 Sight Interpreting for Passages 段落视译练习

Ⓐ **From English to Chinese**

Keep Your Direction

What would you do if you failed? Many people may choose to give up. However, the surest way to success is to keep your direction and stick to your goal. On your way to success, you must keep your direction. It is just like a lamp, guiding you in darkness and helping you overcome obstacles on your way. Otherwise, you will easily get lost or hesitate to go ahead. Direction means objectives. You can get nowhere without an objective in life. You can try to write your objective on paper and make some plans to achieve it. In this way, you will know how to arrange your time and to spend your time properly. And you should also have a belief that you are sure to succeed as long as you keep your direction all the time.

Ⓑ **From Chinese to English**

选秀节目风光不再

一项市场调查表明，中国的电视选秀节目正逐渐失去其对观众的吸引力。

调查显示，新闻、电视剧和大型娱乐节目最受观众欢迎。

上海《新闻晚报》援引央视－索福瑞媒介研究有限公司的话说"去年，选秀类节目的收视率最高，但现在它已失去了统治地位。"

选秀类节目因缺乏创意而遭到批评，湖南卫视的"超女"和"快男"基本上都是"美国偶像"的翻版。

上海《新闻晚报》报道说，选秀节目的过多宣传影响了观众的兴致，而且参加选秀的选手也被批没什么真实才能。

业内专业人士意识到这些批评的声音后，一直在探索能够娱乐观众的新路子。

上海文广新闻传媒集团旗下的东方卫视去年推出了一档名叫"好男儿"的选秀节目。之后，比赛的获胜者还出演了偶像剧《青蛙王子》。但此剧因表演差、情节空洞而遭到炮轰。

调查显示，去年，新闻类节目也很受欢迎，共创造了537亿元的广告收益。

央视－索福瑞媒介研究有限公司经理王兰柱说，电视节目制作人有时低估了观众的欣赏水平，认为照搬照抄也能给节目增色。

他说："很多娱乐节目都是一个模子，会造成观众审美疲劳。"

Unit 8

Festivals & Customs
节日习俗

I. Objectives

After reading this unit, you are required to

☑ practice memory and note-taking techniques.

☑ get familiar with expressions related to festivals and customs.

☑ introduce and talk about holidays and customs in English.

II. Vocabulary Work

1. celebrate   *v.*   庆祝
2. decorate   *v.*   装饰，装点
3. dress up   *v.*   盛装，打扮
4. stay up   *v.*   熬夜
5. champagne   *n.*   香槟酒
6. resolution   *n.*   （新年）愿望
7. present/gift   *n.*   礼物
8. parade   *n.*   游行
9. turkey   *n.*   火鸡
10. dumpling/jiaozi   *n.*   饺子
11. firework   *n.*   烟花，焰火
12. firecracker   *n.*   爆竹
13. festival   *n.*   节日
14. anniversary   *n.*   周年
15. wedding   *n.*   婚礼
16. symbol   *n.*   象征
17. origin   *n.*   起源
18. ceremony   *n.*   仪式，宴会
19. get-together   *n.*   团聚
20. reunion   *n.*   团圆，重聚
21. feast   *n.*   盛宴
22. lantern   *n.*   灯笼
23. staying-up   *n.*   守岁
24. taboo   *n.*   禁忌
25. Ramadan   *n.*   斋月
26. Sabbath   *n.*   安息日
27. Easter   *n.*   复活节
28. Halloween   *n.*   万圣节
29. Carnival   *n.*   狂欢节

III. Phrase Interpreting

A **From English to Chinese**

1. bid farewell to the old year
2. offer sacrifices to one's ancestors
3. family reunion
4. festival air
5. pay a New Year call/visit
6. exchange New Year's greetings
7. The legend has it . . .
8. wait for the coming of the new year

9. I propose a toast to ...

10. special purchases for the Spring Festival

B **From Chinese to English**

1. 庙会
2. 春联
3. 灯谜
4. 贺年片
5. 扫墓
6. 赛龙舟
7. 狮子舞
8. 年夜饭
9. 农历
10. 压岁钱

IV. Sentence Interpreting

A **From English to Chinese**

1. Christmas is just around the corner. How do you usually celebrate it?
2. On Halloween, kids dress up in costumes. They knock on people's doors and ask for candies by saying, "Trick or treat!"
3. A full moon is symbolic of family reunion in China, which is why the Mid-autumn Festival is also known as the "Day of Reunion".
4. In the United States, if you are invited to a friend's house for dinner, it's the custom to bring a small gift, like flowers or dessert.
5. Americans smile mainly to show friendliness. In Japan, people smile when they are sad, happy, apologetic, angry or confused. In traditional Korean culture, smiling means that a person is foolish or thoughtless.

B **From Chinese to English**

1. 祝各位贵宾新年身体健康，事业有成，吉祥如意！
2. 农历五月初五的端午节是纪念古代诗人屈原的日子。
3. 端午节吃粽子、赛龙舟是我们的传统习俗。
4. 值此中秋月明的良宵，我们欢聚一堂，共庆这一中国传统佳节。
5. 值此新春佳节之际，我谨代表公司的全体同仁，感谢各位来宾光临我们的春节联欢晚会。

V. Dialogue Interpreting

Directions: *Interpret the following conversation alternatively into English and Chinese.*

A： 饭菜非常美味可口，雷利夫人，谢谢您的邀请。

B： Well, nobody should have dinner alone today. Thanksgiving is a time for the family and friends to be together. Is this your first Thanksgiving in the United States, Ken?

A： 是的，实际上，我对感恩节了解不多。能否跟我讲讲？我非常感兴趣。

B： Thanksgiving was about the Pilgrims, the first settlers in America. They shared the first harvest with the Indians and gave thanks.

A： 等等，清教徒是谁？

B： They were first immigrants from Europe. And foods we are eating today are the same kinds they ate.

A： 哦，这就是吃火鸡、南瓜饼、玉米的来源。但是为什么感恩节是在 11 月 17 日？

B： It's different every year. But it's always the 4th Thursday of November. Except in Canada, they celebrate it on October. Then in that spirit let each of us give thanks. Each in his own way.

A： 我感谢这一年来身体健康，工作顺利。

B： I give thanks for being here with my family and for being well, so I can enjoy you all.

VI. Text Interpreting

A From English to Chinese

New Year's Eve is an event that is celebrated all over the Western world. On the night of December 31, people will gather together with their friends and family to stay up until midnight, when the old year changes to the new. Ten seconds before midnight, everyone will stop what they are doing and begin to count 10, 9, 8, 7, ..., 3, 2, 1 and then shout "HAPPY NEW YEAR!" This is the time to kiss that special person in your life and to think about all the great things that may happen in the new year.

There are different ways to spend New Year's Eve. Most cities will host a parade. Thousands of people will be together for the celebration. Many times there will be a band playing music, dancing, fireworks and other fun activities for people to choose from. Bars also hold new years' parties, sometimes offering cheap drinks. If a party with just close friends is more up your alley, then you can have a party at your own house with just friends and family.

Another popular tradition is to make New Year's resolutions. Common resolutions are about losing weight, quitting smoking, doing better in school, or becoming a kinder person. Not surprisingly, most people act on their resolutions for only a short time and then stop them. For example, a person who wants to lose weight will often exercise and eat healthy food for only a couple of weeks.

B From Chinese to English

七夕节出现在农历七月七日，又被称为"乞巧节"或"女儿节"。

跟其他地方的一些习俗一样，七夕节是中国传统节日中最具浪漫色彩的一个节日。在七夕节的夜晚，女孩往往会在神殿前摆放一些瓜果供品，以祈求一个幸福美满的婚姻。

关于七夕节的来源很多，其中一个是有关"牛郎"和"织女"的神话故事。他们的浪漫爱情故事在中国民间广为流传。在晴朗的夏夜，天上繁星闪烁，在银河的东西两岸，各有一颗闪亮的星，隔河相望，遥遥相对，那就是牵牛星和织女星。由于这个感人的爱情故事，现代的年轻人把七夕视为中国的情人节。

VII. Enhancement Practice

1 Shadow-speaking in English 英语影子练习

Directions: *Listen to the MP3 and reiterate what you have heard simultaneously.*

I'm Rich Kleinfeldt with some expressions using the word "heart". People believed for a long time that the heart was the center of a person's emotions. That is why the word "heart" is used in so many expressions about emotional situations.

One such expression is to **lose your heart to someone** （爱上，钟情于）. When that happens, you have fallen in love. But if the person who **won your heart** （赢得你的芳心） does not love you, then you are sure to have **a broken heart** （一颗受伤的心）. In your pain and sadness, you may decide that the person you loved is **hard-hearted**. And in fact, has a **heart of stone** （铁石心肠）.

You may decide to **pour out your heart to** （向某人倾诉） a friend. Telling someone about your personal problems can often make you feel better. If your friend does not seem to understand how painful your broken heart is, you may ask her to **have a heart** （发慈悲，做好事）. You are asking your friend to show some sympathy for your situation. Your friend **has her heart in the right place** （真心实意，好心好意） if she says she is sorry, and shows great concern for how you feel.

Your friend may, however, warn you, not to **wear your heart on your sleeve** （流露感情）. In other words, do not let everyone see how lovesick you are. When your heart is on your sleeve, you are showing your deepest emotions. If your friend says **my heart bleeds for you** （怜悯或同情某人）, she means the opposite. She is a **cold-hearted** （铁石心肠） person who does not really care about your situation.

2　Memory & Note-taking 记忆、笔记练习

A　English Passage Retelling

Directions：*This part is to test your short-term memory and note-taking skills. You are required to repeat what you have heard from the recording. You may take notes while you're listening. This passage will be played only once.*

Customs

Every culture has its own rules of what's appropriate and what's not appropriate behavior and serious misunderstandings can occur if we don't know other people's culture rules. And to illustrate my point today, I'm going to give examples from three areas. First, the way people greet each other in different cultures. Second, the way they use names and titles. Third, the way people eat.

OK, let's start with greeting customs. I mean, how people behave when they say hello. First of all, I'm sure you know in the Unites States, or in most Western counties, greetings often involve some sort of touching such as handshake or a hug or a kiss if people know each other very well. On the other hand, people from most Asian countries don't usually feel as comfortable touching in public. Although handshakes between business people are common, many Japanese prefer to bow while people in Thailand normally hold their hands together in a kind of prayer position, like this. So imagine how embarrassing it would be if an American was invited to someone's home in Japan or Thailand and he tried to hug the host. And yet that would be perfectly acceptable in the United States or France or Argentina.

B　Chinese Passage Retelling

Directions：*This part is to test your short-term memory and note-taking skills. You are required to repeat what you have heard from the recording. You may take notes while you're listening. This passage will be played only once.*

送花的礼仪

鲜花，是一种高雅的礼品，通过赠花来表达微妙的感情和心愿，确实别有一番意境。如果懂得一些送花的意义及技巧会更加恰到好处。

（1）给亲友生日送花，对青年人可送玫瑰、月季，中年人可送兰花或茶花，老年人祝寿可送万年青、榕树象征长寿。

（2）给新婚夫妇赠花，最好送玫瑰花或月季花。

（3）给恋人赠花适宜送红玫瑰花、蔷薇花、丁香花或蝴蝶兰。

（4）给友人乔迁之喜赠花可送大方之仙人掌花，寓意乔迁顺利，万事如意。

（5）给病人赠送野百合花，是希望早日康复。

（6）给工商界朋友赠花，可用杜鹃花、大丽花，象征前程万里，事业发达。

（7）新春佳节可送金橘、水仙、百合、状元红、万年青，表达美好的祝愿。

（8）母亲节送康乃馨。

（9）教师节送剑兰、菊花。

（10）芍药花代表离别惦念之意。

3　Numerals 数字练习

Ⓐ 单纯数字听译练

21, 069, 324	10. 6%	9, 261, 369	4. 6%	1, 995	12. 8%	7. 3%
186, 943, 214	4. 2%	1, 305, 678	11. 1%	5. 5%	10. 6%	4, 048, 975
5. 7%	5, 782, 487	3. 7%	11%	15. 6%	5%	5, 963, 211

Ⓑ 带有数字的句子听译练习

1. 据报道，五一劳动节将从过去的七天长假改成三天。

2. 据估计，64% 的游客来自欧洲和北美国家，其余来自亚洲和世界其他地方。

3. 今年前十个月，旅游收入达41亿美元，比起去年同期上升25%。

4. 我本来打算5月26号周四搭乘 BA117 航班抵达，但是现在只能改搭下周四的同班航班。对此延误，深感抱歉！

5. 2002年这种型号的照相机需700美元，现在圣诞节促销，仅售350美元。

4　Idioms Interpreting 习语口译练习

Ⓐ From English to Chinese

1. Do in Rome as the Romans do.

2. Birds of a feather flock together.

3. Cross that bridge when we come to it.

4. Every cloud has a silver lining.

5. Put the cart before the horse.

6. Linked with the same flesh and blood.

7. When disaster strikes, help comes from all sides.

8. Never cast aside and never give up!

9. Take one thing with another.

10. Tastes differ.

B From Chinese to English

1. 猪八戒倒打一耙。
2. 好高骛远。
3. 胆小如鼠。
4. 半斤八两。
5. 大海捞针。
6. 学而优则仕。
7. 梢工多了会翻船。
8. 前不见村，后不着店。
9. 三个臭皮匠胜过诸葛亮。
10. 捡了芝麻，掉了西瓜。

5 Linear Interpreting for Sentences 句子顺译练习

A From English to Chinese

1. May the joy of Christmas be with you throughout the year.
2. Please accept my sincere wishes for the New Year. I hope you will continue to enjoy good health.
3. I'm looking for a Valentine's Day gift for my girlfriend.
4. I know about a Halloween party on Saturday. Would you like to come?
5. I love parades. The Thanksgiving Day parade is always great fun.

B From Chinese to English

1. 明天是国庆节了，假期里你打算干什么？
2. 除夕夜，我们一般吃零食，通宵看电视。
3. 我听说有个很棒的除夕晚会，你会参加吗？
4. 你在圣诞前夜有没有收到什么不错的礼物？
5. 在 1989 年，中国把每年的九月九日定为老人节。

6 Sight Interpreting for Passages 段落视译练习

A From English to Chinese

Christmas is a time for celebration. But this year it is a more sombre occasion for many. Some of those things which could once have been taken for granted suddenly seem less certain, and naturally give rise to feelings of insecurity. People are touched by events which have their roots far across the world. Whether it is the global economy or violence in a distant land, effects can be keenly felt at home.

In such times as these we can all learn some lessons from the past. We might begin to see things in a new perspective. And certainly, we begin to ask ourselves where it is that we can find lasting happiness. Over the years, those who have seemed to me to be the most happy, contented and fulfilled have always been the people who have lived the most outgoing and unselfish lives; the kind of people who are generous with their talents or their time. There are those who use their prosperity or good fortune for the benefit of others.

When life seems hard, the courageous do not lie down and accept defeat, instead they are all the more determined to struggle for a better future. I think we have a huge amount to learn from individuals such as these. And what I believe many of us share with them is a source of strength and peace of mind in our own families and friends.

B From Chinese to English

春节是中国的农历新年，它是中国最重要的传统节日，标志着春天的开始。春节的日期按农历而定，通常出现在公历 2 月上旬的某一天。

春节是一个合家欢聚的日子，出门在外的人总要想方设法在除夕夜到来之前赶回家，吃上一年最重要的一顿"团圆饭"。

大吃大喝历来是春节的主要内容。除了常见的海鲜、家禽和肉类之外，人们还要按各自的地方习俗烹制一些传统菜肴，例如北京的饺子、上海的八宝饭。全国各地都可以见到形态各异、口味不一的年糕。"年糕"这个词里的"糕"字与"高"谐音，寓意来年"节节高"。

Unit 9

Job-hunting & Recruitment
求职招聘

I. Objectives

After reading this unit, you are required to

☑ practice memory techniques and linear interpreting skills.

☑ get familiar with expressions related to job-hunting and recruitment.

☑ equip yourself with languages and skills necessary for a successful job interview.

II. Vocabulary Work

1.	applicant	*n.* 求职者	17.	promotion *n.* 升职
2.	select	*v.* 选拔	18.	prospect *n.* 前景
3.	bonus	*n.* 奖金，额外津贴	19.	qualified *a.* 合格的，胜任的
4.	eligible	*a.* 合格的	20.	qualifications *n.* 资格，先决条件
5.	competitive	*a.* 有竞争力的，竞争的	21.	reference *n.* 证明人
6.	candidate	*n.* 候选人	22.	vacancy/opening *n.* 空职
7.	pension	*n.* 养老金	23.	resume *n.* 简历
8.	fire/dismiss	*v.* 解雇	24.	routine *n./a.* 日常工作（的）
9.	hire/employ	*v.* 雇佣	25.	short-list *v./n.* 列入最后候选
10.	headhunt	*n./v.* 物色人才		人名单
11.	headhunter	*n.* 猎头	26.	salary *n.* 工资
12.	interviewee	*n.* 被面试者	27.	achievement *n.* 成就
13.	interviewer	*n.* 考官，进行面试者	28.	incentive *n./a.* 鼓励（的），
14.	multinational	*n./a.* 跨国公司（的）		奖励（的）
15.	work overtime	*a./n.* 加班（的）	29.	retirement *n.* 退休
16.	position	*n.* 职位	30.	recruit *v.* 录用

III. Phrase Interpreting

A From English to Chinese

1. job interview
2. job description
3. curriculum vitae/resume
4. work overtime
5. job fair
6. job hunting

7. panel interview
8. pay package
9. probationary period
10. project manager

B From Chinese to English

1. 全职工作
2. 职业培训
3. 工作职责
4. 求职信
5. 频繁更换工作，跳槽
6. 责任感
7. 高薪工作
8. 带薪假期
9. 人才市场
10. 人力资源部

IV. Sentence Interpreting

A From English to Chinese

1. I'd like to know something about you. Could you tell me a bit about your education? What was your major when you were studying in university?
2. What unique experience or qualifications separate you from other candidates?
3. My graduate school training combined with my internship should qualify me for this particular job. I am sure I will be successful.
4. I studied in a university for four years. There I majored in foreign trade. Then I continued studying for a MA degree with the same major.
5. I'm curious why you'd like to leave your present company and join us.

B From Chinese to English

1. 你的五年目标是什么？你打算如何实现这个目标？
2. 请描述你现在的工作。你觉得这份工作最有意义的部分是什么？
3. 我喜欢这份工作具有挑战性。我的潜能得到了全面的发挥。我在这个领域的经验更加丰富了。
4. 你能承受工作上的压力吗？你的英文流利吗？你工作上取得的最大成就是什么？
5. 我负责回复电子邮件和接听电话。我工作职责的另外一部分是组织研讨会。我组织演讲者，邀请客人，并安排会址和住宿等有关事宜。

V. Dialogue Interpreting

Directions：*Interpret the following conversation alternatively into English and Chinese.*

　F：　上午好，李先生。请坐。

M： Thank you. Mrs. Jones.

F： 您的简历做得很好。您能否做个自我介绍？

M： Well，I think I'm a serious-minded man. I'm calm and I don't panic in the crisis. I like jokes and have a good sense of humor. And also I enjoy working with all kinds of people. I even like people who are bad-tempered or something like that.

F： 这很有趣。您未来五年的目标是什么？

M： Well，I see myself in the public relations and I hope I can keep climbing the career ladder in this field.

F： 您为什么想离职加入我们公司？

M： Well，first of all，I want to leave my present employers because I don't see any development for myself in this company. The job I'm doing now is a kind of routine and secretarial type of work. And I know your company is a large company，which has a good reputation. The work will be more challenging，and I would have more scope and opportunity in your company so that I can use my initiatives.

F： 我想知道您的优点和缺点是什么？

M： Strengths and weaknesses? Well，as I mentioned before，I think my sense of humor and my ability to work with all types of people is a particular strength. My weaknesses? I suppose I'm a bit of a perfectionist. I'm quite often dissatisfied with what I've done. I always think I can do it better or in a different way.

F： 我不认为这是缺点。我会把它看作是优点。现在，您有什么其他问题想问我吗？

M： Yes，if I get this job，would I be able to work abroad in one of your overseas branches?

F： 是的，当然可以。我们的员工会定期去其他分部进行为期六个月的实习。

M： Oh，that's very good.

F： 好的，恐怕时间紧急，谢谢您今天来参加面试。本周末我们会与您联系。

M： Thank you for seeing me.

VI. Text Interpreting

A **From English to Chinese**

The key to taking part in a successful interview is preparation. Before you attend the interview，be sure to find out the important facts about the company，its main activities，products and services. If you spend some time doing this homework，the interview is much more likely to be successful. Many candidates fail to do this thoroughly，so if you are well-informed，you will look better than many other applicants. You can get most of the information from the company website.

It goes without saying that you should arrive for the interview on time. That means knowing the exact location and how long it will take you to get there. If you arrive late and out of breath, you will make a very poor impression.

You also need to prepare questions to ask the interviewer. You should see the interview as a two-way process, partly for you to make sure that the job will give you the career development that you want. After all, if the company doesn't suit you, it is better to find this out at the interview, rather than after you have accepted the job. Besides, if you ask intelligent questions, the interviewer will be impressed by your knowledge and interest in the company.

Finally, remember that the interviewer may ask other people for their opinions of you. This means that you need to make a good impression on the employees who show you around or the receptionist as well. If they feel that you are impolite, probably the interviewer will hear about it.

B **From Chinese to English**

您好，我的名字是张佳。我来自山东的青岛。但是三岁的时候我随家人搬到北京。我在北京长大。大约三年前我中学毕业，现在我在这个城市就读大学。我现在大三，主修经济学，辅修西班牙语。而且，我还在杂货店兼职做出纳。生活非常忙碌，但是我闲暇时间喜欢远足、读书或和朋友玩。毕业后，我想在这个地区的贸易公司工作。

VII. Enhancement Practice

1 Shadow-speaking in English 英语影子练习

Directions: *Listen to the MP3 and reiterate what you have heard simultaneously.*

China's Ministry of Human Resources and Social Security started a weeklong job-hunting service campaign on Sunday to help university graduates get employed amid the global financial crisis.

Statistics showed that about six million students will graduate from universities and colleges next year and some 800, 000 of this year's graduates are still awaiting job offers.

Si Yilei, director of the ministry's National Center for Human Resources, said besides the job fairs, the ministry would also provide consultations on job-hunting, give guidance and training to the graduates who choose to start their own business, and establish a database of unemployed graduates.

Vice Minister Zhang Xiaojian said the graduates would face severe challenge in job-hunting due to the global financial crisis.

More job opportunities in less-developed central and western parts of China will be offered to the graduates, he said.

2 Memory & Note-taking 记忆、笔记练习

A English Passage Retelling

Directions: *This part is to test your short-term memory and note-taking skills. You are required to repeat what you have heard from the recording. You may take notes while you're listening. This passage will be played only once.*

Changing Job Market

If you will be graduating from high school or college in the next year or two, I know you are very concerned about your future. Probably the most important questions on your mind are these: Will you find a good job? And what should you do to make sure that you will? To help you answer these questions, first I am going to describe how the US job market has changed in the past 100 years. After that I will tell you what you can do to prepare yourself for the job market today.

OK, now first of all, to begin, let's talk about the American job market and how it has changed. Without any question, the most important change in the 20th century was the shift, the uh, change from a manufacturing economy to a service economy ... You can see this clearly if you take a look at the graph on job restructuring (重组). Let's look at those statistics. You can see that the percentage of manufacturing jobs has gone down dramatically since the beginning of the 20th century, and it will continue to decrease in the 21st century. And what about service jobs? At the same time the percentage of manufacturing jobs has gone down, and there has been a great increase in the percentage of service jobs. Basically, 100 years ago, 80% of workers worked in agriculture or manufacturing; but today, as we start the 21st century, only about 20% do, while 80% provide services. And you can see that by the year 2020, the percentage of service workers will increase to 90%; in other words, within 20 years, nine out of ten workers in the United States will supply services and not products.

B Chinese Passage Retelling

Directions: *This part is to test your short-term memory and note-taking skills. You are required to repeat what you have heard from the recording. You may take notes while you're listening. This passage will be played only once.*

美国十大最不受欢迎的工作

一、餐厅领班

该职业被美国人认为并不具有太大价值，除非只是为了吸取经验，打算以后到一家著名的餐馆或酒店任职。

二、柜台服务员

餐厅和咖啡馆的柜台服务员工作量惊人，日薪理应较高，但现实并非如此。

三、剧院引座员、大堂服务员、检票员

在剧院工作时间不正常、薪酬低，又要应付脾气不好的观众，并不划算。

四、服装打板师

工时长，工资低，工作单调，索然无味。

五、护卫

选择护卫等保安行业作为暑期工或许很好，但并不被认为是长远之计。

六、服务生

该行业的生计很多时候取决于顾客。

七、导游

如果喜欢外出旅游及为游客当向导，这份工作就非常适合，否则最好另谋高就，因为在美国，该职位被认为福利微薄。

八、模特儿、产品示范员及推销员

除非能跻身顶级模特儿的行列或者当上《叫对价》（*The Price Is Right*）的主持，否则致富的机会等于零。

九、洗碗工

靠洗碗为生，会伤害到手部皮肤，甚至容易被热水烫伤，该职业工资低而且没有小费可收。

十、电影放映员

可以免费看新片是挺好的，但要连续看上几十次就会十分枯燥。美国电影放映员的工资和福利都很微薄。

3　Numerals 数字听译练习

A 单纯数字听译练习

545, 760	485, 255	6, 131, 002	3, 481, 991	6, 844, 521
854, 166	322, 752	5, 530, 067	7, 573, 658	6, 057, 331
3/4	5/8	37/65	1/3	4.579

B 带有数字的句子听译练习

1. 在美国 30% 的工人因为缺少教育或培训，每小时的薪酬不到 8 美金。

2. 这个清单列出的 25 个职业中，有 18 个要求的最低学位是学士。

3. 2004 年 3 月至 2005 年 11 月，美国把 50 多万的生产工作机会迁移到亚洲，因为这里的劳动力低廉。

4. 新加坡总共有 11.5% 的劳动力属于专业人士或技术工人，比如会计、工程师和律师。

5. 现在超过 80% 的工作都是在网上申请的。人力资源主管不愿麻烦归档众多求职信，所以以平信方式寄来的都被直接扔进了垃圾筒。

4 Idioms Interpreting 习语口译练习

A From English to Chinese

1. stop and smell the roses
2. He who takes charge knows the responsibility.
3. frankly speaking
4. Dog eat dog.
5. put all of one's eggs in one basket
6. Tears are the silent language of grief.
7. The battle is to the strong.
8. The best of friends must part.
9. The busiest men find（or have）the most leisure（or time）.
10. The early bird catches the worm.

B From Chinese to English

1. 破釜沉舟。
2. 弱不禁风。
3. 纸上谈兵。
4. 老调重弹。
5. 初出茅庐。
6. 悬梁刺股。
7. 三思而后行。
8. 情人眼里出西施。
9. 吃一堑，长一智。
10. 知无不言，言无不尽。

5 Linear Interpreting for Sentences 句子顺译练习

A From English to Chinese

1. Good morning! I'm Amy Huang. I have an appointment with Mr. Wilson.

2. What are your salary requirements? What kind of salary are you looking for?

3. What did you enjoy most at school? What was the course that you enjoyed most?

4. Money is important, but the responsibility that goes along with this job is what interests me the most.

5. I'm very fond of drawing. And I have a great interest in traditional Chinese paintings.

B From Chinese to English

1. 你怎样形容你的个性?

2. 我擅长与人沟通。我责任感强。

3. 你目前工作上碰到过的最大的问题是什么，你是怎样解决这个问题的?

4. 2003 年我毕业于华东师范大学。

5. 我负责招聘工作。我工作的职责还包括培训员工。

6　Sight Interpreting for Passages 段落视译练习

A From English to Chinese

There comes a time in everyone's life when they start dreading Monday morning. Once, every day brought new challenges and experiences. Now as far as your job's concerned, you've been there, seen it and done it too. It's time to move on. But before you resign, ask yourself if there isn't scope to learn and develop within your current job. Tell your employer you're dissatisfied. They may have a long-term development plan for you — or there may be a chance of a pay rise or promotion. You should always abandon the short-term gains for the long-term benefits of future career success.

Ok, so you've found a new job that offers greater satisfaction and long-term personal development. That still leaves the sharp issue of salary. Negotiating a salary is a two-way conversation. You wan to fill the position; the new employer wants the position filled. At all times, you'll need to focus on your strengths and your skills and aim for a salary that represents your value. The first figure you mention probably won't be the figure you agree on, but it is a figure from which will only negotiate down. The key is to negotiate from a position of strength. In other words, you have to believe that you are bringing something to the table.

B From Chinese to English

　　鲍勃在公司干了 6 年后最终被解雇了。其实他没有犯错，相反，他是一名很好的员工，可是公司正在裁减人员。20 世纪 90 年代末，这非常普遍，因此一些职业专家针对如何保住饭碗提出了一些策略。

确保每个人都认识你。有时，做一名好员工不如让别人知道你是一名好员工重要。主动要求新的工作职责，推销自己的观点，总而言之，让别人了解你。

学习能让你更加胜任这份工作的知识。如果公司买了新电脑，就去学习如何使用。如果学习更多的营销知识能够有所帮助，就去报名参加营销速成班。

确保你对公司了如指掌，并好好利用这个信息。如果发现销售成为公司最重要的部分，试着朝着销售的领域发展。

要积极乐观。满腹牢骚的人总是不如喜爱称赞的人受欢迎。

提高说和写的技巧。你有好的主意还不够，还需要能够表达自己的观点。

打动你的老板。早到晚退，着装职业，尽管其他人穿得很休闲。这总是能够给老板留下好印象。

最后，一切都归结于一个基本的策略：给自己增值，这样公司就不想失去你。

Unit 10

Business Etiquette
商务礼仪

I. Objectives

After reading this unit, you are required to

☑ practice memory and shadow-speaking techniques.

☑ get familiar with expressions related to business etiquettes.

☑ apply the theory of business etiquettes in English.

II. Vocabulary Work

1. etiquette   *n.*   礼仪
2. anticipate   *v.*   预见，期待
3. banquet   *n.*   酒席，正式的宴会
4. regards   *n.*   问候，致意
5. consensus   *n.*   一致的意见，共识
6. negotiation   *n.*   协商，谈判
7. compromise   *n.*   妥协，折中，和解
8. agenda   *n.*   议程
9. persuade   *v.*   说服，劝服
10. prompt   *a.*   准时的，按时的
11. compliment   *n.*   赞扬，恭维
12. modest   *a.*   谦逊的，适度的
13. eloquent   *a.*   口才好的，雄辩的
14. hilarious   *a.*   狂欢的，令人捧腹的
15. distinguished   *a.*   卓越的，杰出的

16. embrace   *n./v.*   拥抱
17. farewell   *n.*   一路平安，再见，告别
18. gossip   *n.*   闲话，流言
19. greeting   *n.*   致敬，问候
20. get-together   *n.*   聚会
21. protocol   *n.*   外交礼仪，草约
22. feast   *n.*   盛宴
23. appointment   *n.*   约会，约定
24. agreement   *n.*   同意，协议
25. courtesy   *n.*   礼貌，礼仪，殷勤
26. offensive   *a.*   令人不快的，冒犯的
27. nosy   *a.*   好管闲事的，爱打听的
28. hug   *n./v.*   拥抱，紧抱
29. lavish   *a.*   过分大方的，浪费的
30. salute   *v.*   向……打招呼

III. Phrase Interpreting

A **From English to Chinese**

1. diplomatic etiquette
2. return dinner
3. in one's own name
4. Take care!
5. be one's voice
6. enter into negotiation
7. people from all walks of life
8. I have the honour to call upon . . .

9. declare ... open   10. celebration remarks

B From Chinese to English

1. 名片   2. 餐桌礼仪
3. 握手   4. 同行间的礼仪，行规
5. 大吃大喝   6. 友好使者
7. 接风   8. 饯行
9. 茶话会   10. 对……进行友好访问

IV. Sentence Interpreting

A From English to Chinese

1. Here is a copy of the itinerary we have worked out for you and your friends. Would you please have a look at it?
2. Tips are not usually added to the check. They are not included in the price of the meal，either.
3. You're going out of your way for us，I believe.
4. I wonder if it is possible to arrange shopping for us after our visit.
5. I am pleased to join the honorable Mayor of New York as well as other dignitaries here today for this exciting event.

B From Chinese to English

1. 在我们正式开始前，大家喝点什么吧。
2. 希望你能告诉我们，要不然我们无法确定你想要的是什么。
3. 直接上门推销产品的销售人员在某种程度上已经侵犯了公民的私生活。
4. 我希望这次来参观没有给你们增添太多的麻烦。
5. 我此行的目的正是想探询与贵公司建立贸易关系的可能性。

V. Dialogue Interpreting

Directions：*Interpret the following conversation alternatively into English and Chinese.*

  A：This is the first time I've been in China，and everything here fascinated me. But there is something I can never figure out!

  B：什么事情？有什么令你迷惑的？说出来看看我能不能帮上你的忙。

  A：Good! You turn up so timely! I am just expecting some good explanation. You know the other day one of my Chinese friends was celebrating his birthday so I asked him what he would like for a birthday present. Do you know what he said? "No, no! Don't give me anything. Don't be polite!" Can you believe it?

B： 事实上，我相信他是这么说的，这只是中国式的客气和矜持。通常情况下，他并不是真的表示拒绝，除非他坚持不要，中国人一般给人帮过忙或者是关系亲密的朋友之间才接受馈赠，他们不想让朋友们破费，也就是花钱。

A： What did he mean by refusing to accept a present from me then?

B： 我认为他并不是真的拒绝接受你的礼物。那只是他表达客气的方式而已。他不是故意无礼，当然他也不是想要冒犯你。

A： Well, how do you like that? And what was I supposed to do or say in such a situation?

B： 首先你要明白的是中国人在有些情况下并不是很直接的，在这种情况下你必须一再坚持，如果对方是位老先生，你还得多次坚持，但即使那样，我怀疑他也不会给你一个直接的答复。或者你可以直接买好礼物而不必问他，不管你买什么，他肯定会高兴的，毕竟重要的是你的一份心意。

A： So you mean buying a gift is a better choice than not, right?

B： 我是这样认为的。

A： Thank you.

 VI. Text Interpreting

A **From English to Chinese**

It is often said that politeness costs nothing. In fact, it seems that a little more courtesy could save businesses £5 billion every year.

Frequently hearing the phrase "thank you" or "well done" means the same to staff as a modest pay rise, researchers say.

Praise and encouragement also makes employees more likely to work hard and stay in their jobs, saving on the cost of finding replacements.

A third of 1,000 workers surveyed by consulting firm White Water Strategies said they did not get thanked at all when they did well — and a further third said they were not thanked enough.

In both cases, staff said they felt undervalued, meaning they were less likely to exert themselves and were more likely to look for employment elsewhere.

The net result is around £5.2 billion in lost productivity from employees who would raise their game if they felt more appreciated, White Water claimed.

According to the company, praising staff has the same motivational kick as a 1 percent pay rise — and works out much cheaper for bosses.

Three out of four employees said that regular acknowledgement by their bosses was important to them, but only a quarter said they were actually given as much praise as they felt they needed.

Psychologist Averil Leimon, a director of White Water Strategies, said that words of praise did more than create a pleasant place to work — they could even boost profits.

B **From Chinese to English**

主席先生，女士们，先生们：

我很荣幸地宣布国际贸易合作会议开幕。我谨代表中国政府和人民，还有我个人，向大会表示热烈的祝贺并热忱地欢迎所有的客人和代表。

这次大会得到商务部的大力支持，我能够在这次国际大会上致辞确实非常荣幸和愉快。我相信我们的共同努力一定会取得丰硕的成果并将直接促进进一步的贸易扩大，这对我们两国都是有益的。

希望大会圆满成功。

谢谢大家。

VII. Enhancement Practice

1 Shadow-speaking in English 英语影子练习

Directions: *Listen to the MP3 and reiterate what you have heard simultaneously.*

(Mark and Amanda are talking about table manners.)

Mike: You've got to try these sausages, Amanda. They're delicious!

Amanda: I'd love to eat a sausage, Mike, but didn't your mother ever teach you any table manners? You shouldn't talk with your mouth full! No one wants to see what your food looks like when it's all chewed up, and besides, I think you just spit something in my eye!

Mike: Sorry! Sometimes I just get excited about something and then I forget my manners. While we're on the topic, though, is there anything else I need to be aware of?

Amanda: First of all, you should sit with better posture when you're eating. You shouldn't put your elbows on the dinner table, and you definitely shouldn't be all slouched over — that's just rude. Also, when you're having a meal with relatives or family friends, you should always wait for your elders to start eating first before you take anything for yourself.

Mike: Wow, maybe I should just call you "Miss Manners" from now on. How did you become such an expert on this subject anyway?

Amanda: I don't know if I'm an "expert", but my parents were always very strict about this kind of thing when I was growing up. Weren't yours?

Mike： ... Hold on! I'll answer you as soon as I finish swallowing my food!

2 Memory & Note-taking 记忆、笔记练习

Ⓐ English Passage Retelling

Directions：*This part is to test your short-term memory and note-taking skills. You are required to repeat what you have heard from the recording. You may take notes while you're listening. This passage will be played only once.*

Meeting New People

People from different cultures sometimes do things that make each other uncomfortable — sometimes without even realizing it.

Most Americans have never been out of the country and have very little experience with foreigners. But they are usually spontaneous, friendly and open, and enjoy meeting new people, having guests and bringing people together formally or informally. They tend to use first names in most situations and speak freely about themselves. So if your American hosts do something that makes you uncomfortable, try to let them know how you feel. Most people will appreciate your honesty and try not to make you feel uncomfortable again.

Many travelers find it easier to meet people in the United States than in other countries. They may just come up and introduce themselves or even invite you over before they really know you. Sometimes Americans are said to be superficially friendly. Perhaps it seems so, but they are probably just having a good time. Just like anywhere else, it takes time to become real friends with people in the United States.

When you stay with American friends, they will probably enjoy introducing you to their friends and family. They usually make a point of trying to make you feel comfortable and relaxed. On the whole, they tend to be informal. Men shake hands, but usually only when they are introduced. When a woman and a man are introduced, shaking hands is up to the woman. Americans rarely shake hands to say good-bye, except on business occasions.

House guests may bring gifts when they come to visit, and they often offer to help in some ways. As a guest, you may want to ask your host or hostess if there's anything you can do to help in the kitchen. In many cases, the gesture is more important than actually.

B **Chinese Passage Retelling**

Directions： *This part is to test your short-term memory and note-taking skills. You are required to repeat what you have heard from the recording. You may take notes while you're listening. This passage will be played only once.*

接受别人的名片的注意事项

名片是一个人身份的象征，当前已成为人们社交活动的重要工具。因此，名片的递送、接受、存放也讲究社交礼仪。

名片的递送。在社交场合，名片是自我介绍的简便方式。交换名片的顺序一般是："先客后主，先低后高"。当与多人交换名片时，应依照职位高低的顺序，或是由近及远，依次进行，切勿跳跃式地进行，以免对方误认为有厚此薄彼之感。递送时应将名片正面面向对方，双手奉上。眼睛应注视对方，面带微笑，并大方地说："这是我的名片，请多多关照。"名片的递送应在介绍之后，在尚未弄清对方身份时不应急于递送名片，更不要把名片视同传单随便散发。

名片的接受。接受名片时应起身，面带微笑注视对方。接过名片时应说："谢谢"，随后有一个微笑阅读名片的过程，阅读时可将对方的姓名职街念出声来，并抬头看看对方的脸，使对方产生一种受重视的满足感。然后，回敬一张本人的名片，如身上未带名片，应向对方表示歉意。在对方离去之前，或话题尚未结束，不必急于将对方的名片收藏起来。

名片的存放。接过别人的名片切不可随意摆弄或扔在桌子上，也不要随便地塞在口袋里或丢在包里，应放在西服左胸的内衣袋或名片夹里，以示尊重。

3 Numerals 数字听译练习

A 单纯数字听译练习

100, 001	100, 099	107, 088	198, 456	453, 629
702, 078	888, 888	1, 234, 567	8, 976, 823	5, 406, 301
7, 896, 098	9, 011, 252	3, 286, 135	12, 345, 678	56, 853, 007
150, 000, 000	709, 875, 312	1, 000, 000, 000	10, 000, 000, 000	

B 带有数字的句子听译练习

1. 这个工厂投资 1 200 万元，修建了一栋 26 层居住面积 48 000 平方米的公寓大楼。

2. 目前世界总人口达到 64 亿 6 470 万。

3. 在我国有 6 000 万人是残疾人。

4. 2007 年，全国高等学校在校生总数为 2 700 万人，其中研究生 119 万 5 000 人。

5. 1949 年至 1998 年，中国的粮食总产量由 1.1 亿吨增加到 5.1 亿吨，增长 3.5 倍，年平均增长 3.1% ，是人口增长率的 2.5 倍。

4 Idioms Interpreting 习语口译练习

A From English to Chinese

1. pick up the evil by the root
2. Nothing is impossible for a willing heart.
3. God helps those who help themselves.
4. Homer sometimes nods.
5. add fuel to the flames
6. draw a cake to satisfy one's hunger
7. as thin as a shadow
8. have a card up one's sleeve
9. The eye is blind if the mind is absent.
10. The fool has his heart on his tongue, the wise man keeps his tongue in his heart.

B From Chinese to English

1. 盛气凌人。
2. 竭尽全力。
3. 如履薄冰。
4. 挥金如土。
5. 见风使舵。
6. 眼中钉。
7. 昙花一现。
8. 千钧一发。
9. 进退维谷。
10. 蠢人嘴巴讲，聪明人用心想。

5 Linear Interpreting for Sentences 句子顺译练习

A From English to Chinese

1. As a host, it's your responsibility to choose an appropriate restaurant, taking care as much as possible ahead of time such as arranging for how to pay the bill and reserving a nice table.
2. Tomorrow the delegation will leave for Shanghai. I'd like to wish you all a pleasant trip.
3. The general rules for greetings are gentlemen/young men/the employees say hello first to ladies/elderly men/the employers.
4. I particularly want to pay tribute to our Chinese partners without whose effort it would have been impossible for us to reach the successful conclusion of our cooperative

agreements.

5. May I take this opportunity to outline our history, and our strategy towards the Chinese market.

B **From Chinese to English**

1. 现在，我愉快地宣布"拉萨城市建设国际研讨会"开幕。
2. 2008 年，对于中国人民来说是很不寻常、很不平凡的一年。
3. 约翰逊先生，我想借此机会向您表示感谢，谢谢您诚挚的邀请。
4. 我很高兴和大家一起庆祝蓝天职业学院建校 50 周年。
5. 如果客户是为商务目的而来，主人要起身接待客人，给他让一个座位并且倒上一杯咖啡。当客人起身告辞时，主人需将客人送到门口或者电梯口。

6 Sight Interpreting for Passages 段落视译练习

A **From English to Chinese**

It is fair to say that the Number One pastime in China is eating.

Banquets are usually held in restaurants in private rooms that have been reserved for the purpose. You will be met at the door and led to the banquet room. Traditionally, the head of your delegation should enter the room first. Do not be surprised if your hosts greet you with a loud round of applause. The proper response is to applaud back.

Seating arrangements are stricter than in the West. Guests should never assume that they may sit where they please and should wait for hosts to guide them to their places. Traditionally, the Chinese regard the right side as the superior and the left side as the inferior. Therefore on formal occasions, the host invariably arranges for the main guests to sit on his right side.

It is the host's responsibility to serve the guests, and at very formal banquets people do not begin to eat until the host has served a portion to the principal guest. Or, the host may simply raise his chopsticks and announce that eating has begun. After this point, one may serve oneself any food in any amount. Remember to go slow on eating. Don't fill yourself up when five courses are left to go. To stop eating in the middle of a banquet is rude, and your host may incorrectly think that something has been done to offend you.

Drinking takes an important place in Chinese banquets. It is likely that the host will stand and hold his glass out with both hands while saying a few words. When he says the words "gan bei", which means bottoms up, all present should drain their glasses. After this initial toast, drinking and toasting are open to all. No words are needed to make a toast, and it is not necessary to drain your glass, although to do so is more respectful. When filling another's glass, it is polite to fill it as full as you can. This symbolizes full respect and friendship.

B From Chinese to English

　　一位美国朋友邀请你去他家。你以前从未去过美国人的家，你不确定该怎么做。该带一个礼物吗？该怎么穿？该几点到？到了那里该做什么？很高兴你发问。你若是客人，只要使自己感到自在就好了。待客之道就是这样：虽然不在家，却让客人有宾至如归的感觉。

　　是否带礼物的问题常使客人不安。在某些文化中，送主人礼物不只是社交礼节——还是必要的。但是在美国文化中，客人并不一定要带礼物。当然，有些人的确会带个表示感谢的小礼物给他们的主人。一般来说，花和糖果都是适宜的礼物，如果这家有小孩，就可以送玩具。如果你不打算带礼物，别担心，甚至没有人会注意到你的空手而来。

　　美国人的待客之道从家里开始——尤其和食物有关。大多数美国人都同意，无论如何，好的家常菜胜过餐馆的菜。受邀吃饭时，你或许可以问："需要我带些什么吗？"除非是每人带一道菜的聚餐，否则主人很可能会回答："不用，你来就可以了。"大多数非正式的聚餐，你应该穿舒适、轻便的衣服。设法准时到，否则打电话告诉主人你会晚点到。用餐时，习惯上人们会称赞女主人烹调的美食。当然，最大的赞美是多吃！

Unit 11

Corporate Image
企业形象

I. Objectives

After reading this unit, you are required to

☑ practice memory and shadow-speaking techniques.

☑ get familiar with expressions related to coporate image.

☑ present topics about corporate image in English.

II. Vocabulary Work

1. ethics	*n.*	道德标准	16. downsize	*v.*	裁减
2. promotion	*n.*	晋升	17. recruitment	*n.*	招聘
3. discipline	*n.*	纪律	18. marketing	*n.*	营销
4. patent	*n.*	专利	19. globalization	*n.*	全球性，全球化
5. value	*n.*	价值观	20. operation	*n.*	经营
6. identification	*n.*	标志	21. fidelity	*n.*	忠实，忠诚
7. market-oriented	*a.*	以市场为导向	22. strategy	*n.*	战略，策略
8. concept	*n.*	理念	23. trustworthy	*a.*	值得信赖的，可靠的
9. competitor	*n.*	竞争对手			
10. corporate	*a.*	法人（组织）的，公司的	24. subsidiary	*n.*	子公司
			25. merger	*n.*	合并
11. board	*n.*	董事会	26. vision	*n.*	目光，眼力，远见
12. innovation	*n.*	创新	27. bottleneck	*n.*	瓶颈
13. shareholders	*n.*	股东	28. teamwork	*n.*	合作，协同工作
14. logo	*n.*	标识	29. norm	*n.*	规范
15. standardization	*n.*	标准化	30. orientation	*n.*	定位

III. Phrase Interpreting

Ⓐ **From English to Chinese**

1. corporate identity
2. corporate image
3. enterprise objective
4. customer loyalty
5. corporate logo
6. brand image

7. product concept

9. brand enhancing

8. habitual buying

10. social acceptability

B From Chinese to English

1. 评估标准

3. 全国性品牌

5. 形象广告

7. 成长期

9. 创品牌

2. 成熟期

4. 跨国公司

6. 管理多样性

8. 团队精神

10. 公司文化，企业文化

IV. Sentence Interpreting

A From English to Chinese

1. We sincerely welcome people of all walks of life both at home and abroad to join, in whatever form, the partnership with the corporation in its business operation.

2. A key factor in building a strong corporate image is consistency.

3. The company is hoping to increase public trust in its products through its affiliation with the established and respected Olympics movement.

4. Obviously we might not be able to get the return overnight, but we believe this has to be Samsung's long-term commitment to the worldwide consumers who we serve, and over time we would like to build the consumer's affinity.

5. While the costs of sponsoring the Olympics may seem excessive, these companies are competing in a global market.

B From Chinese to English

1. 该公司将竭诚与客户建立互惠互利的合作关系，坦诚相待，共同发展商务旅游事业。

2. 我们已建立了一张遍布世界各地100多个国家和地区的发行网络。

3. 从创造一个标识或公司品牌开始是很明智的，因为企业形象的发展要依靠它们。

4. 麦当劳奇迹的魅力并不是来自食物，而是来自服务。

5. 在产品制作上，麦当劳最引以为自豪的是完全标准化的过程和食品口味给顾客带来的无限依赖感和安全感。

V. Dialogue Interpreting

Directions: *Interpret the following conversation alternatively into English and Chinese.*

A： 随着知识经济的到来，市场竞争的脚步已跨越了价格竞争、质量竞争和服务竞争的阶段，企业已经进入形象竞争的时代。

B： Well, the idea may sound a little bit strange, but it does make sense. The corporate image will make the company identifiable and different from the rest and it will also determine its importance in the business world.

A： 大型企业的形象战略已做得比较充分，人们耳熟能详的都是可口可乐、惠普、诺思通、佳能、家乐福、柯达等大型企业。

B： Yes, but the well-established corporations have come a long way in maintaining a good corporate image.

A： 为了创造一个企业形象，企业应该始终一致，而这一点是很难做到的。

B： Well, yes, actually. A number of multinationals have taken solid steps in an attempt to recover from negative images of corruption and reports of abusing cheap labor. French retail giant Carrefour has opened a 24-hour hotline to hear reports on staff corruption crimes. The decision was made after eight Chinese managers were detained by police in corruption probes the week before.

A： 我听说麦当劳已经为95%的中国员工增加了工资。这一举动是针对大量的强烈抗议进行的，抗议指出在中国南方城市广州麦当劳付给兼职员工的工资比当地法定最低工资低了40%。

B： The local people believe that these measures will make the business transactions more fair and transparent.

A： 随着中国监管系统的发展，人民社会不公正意识的增加，仅依靠公众关系来建立公司形象已经不够了。中国的法律系统正在更新工业标准，并且正在赶上国际标准。

VI. Text Interpreting

Ⓐ From English to Chinese

Whether you love or hate your company's annual holiday office party, it may not even happen this year.

As a financial crisis roils world markets and fears of a deep global recession grow, about one-fifth of US businesses are saying "no" to end-of-year festivities this holiday season, according to a survey released on Monday.

If you're one of the lucky ones to keep on celebrating, be aware that only 71 percent of companies are offering booze this year — a cruel and unusual punishment, perhaps.

"We've always looked at this as the year-end economic barometer," said Battalia Winston Amrop Chief Executive Dale Winston. "People will still have parties, but it's the mood of the country — the mood of the country is not a celebratory mood. "

This year, only 81 percent of companies are throwing a party, fewer than during the holiday season that followed the 2001 attacks on the World Trade Center and the Pentagon, or during the recession of 1991.

Some 37 percent of companies blamed the economy for more modest party plans this year, the survey found, nearly double the number from last year.

B **From Chinese to English**

2008 年，在北京奥林匹克体育场的上空漂浮着一个巨大的、色彩艳丽的龙形气球，它象征着中国的传统文化和力量。当气球靠近时，它喷出的火焰将点燃奥林匹克圣火。现在这还只是 Naoki Nishi 脑中的一个想法而已，但这个想法很有可能成为现实。他在广岛拥有一家名为 Show 公司的企业。

目前 Show 公司在日本有 16 名员工，而中国作为生产基地有 71 名员工。在日本，该公司已经垄断大型特色充气气球市场。2002 年在横滨举行的世界杯闭幕仪式上，Nishi 打败 250 多家竞标公司，在一分钟之内用 25 个鼓风机吹起一个富士山造型的气球，高达 20 米。公司也向佛罗里达州的迪士尼乐园出租载人热气球，这在那些陪孩子来的老人中是很受欢迎的。

VII. Enhancement Practice

1　Shadow-speaking in English 英语影子练习

Directions: *Listen to the MP3 and reiterate what you have heard simultaneously*

The Google Culture

Though growing rapidly, Google still maintains a small company feel. At the Googleplex headquarters almost everyone eats in the Google café (known as "Charlie's Place"), sitting at whatever table, has an opening and enjoying conversations with Googlers from all different departments. Topics range from the trivial to the technical, and whether the discussion is about computer games or encryption or ad serving software, it's not surprising to hear someone say, "That's a product I helped develop before I came to Google. "

Google's emphasis on innovation and commitment to cost containment means each employee is a hands-on contributor. There's little in the way of corporate hierarchy and everyone wears several hats. The international webmaster who creates Google's holiday logos spent a week translating the entire site into Korean. The chief operations engineer is also a licensed neurosurgeon. Because everyone realizes they are an equally important part

of Google's success, no one hesitates to skate over a corporate officer during roller hockey.

Google's hiring policy is aggressively non-discriminatory and favors ability over experience. The result is a staff that reflects the global audience the search engine serves. Google has offices around the globe and Google engineering centers are recruiting local talent in locations from Zurich to Bangalore. Dozens of languages are spoken by Google staffers, from Turkish to Telugu. When not at work, Googlers pursue interests from cross-country cycling to wine tasting, from flying to frisbee. As Google expands its development team, it continues to look for those who share an obsessive commitment to creating search perfection and having a great time doing it.

2 Memory & Note-taking 记忆、笔记练习

Ⓐ **English Passage Retelling**

Directions: *This part is to test your short-term memory and note-taking skills. You are required to repeat what you have heard from the recording. You may take notes while you're listening. This passage will be played only once.*

Corporate Image

Haier is the world's fourth largest white goods manufacturer and is the official home appliances sponsor of the Beijing 2008 Olympic Games.

As of 2007, the Haier Group has established a total of 64 trading companies (19 located overseas), 29 manufacturing plants (24 overseas), 8 design centers (5 overseas) and 16 industrial parks (4 overseas). Consistent with Haier's position as a global brand, the company employs over 50,000 people around the world. In addition, Haier boasts a strong sales network totaling 58,800 which last year accounted for a global turnover of 118 billion RMB (16.2 billion USD).

Guided by the branding strategy of CEO Zhang Ruimin, Haier has advanced through the "brand building", "diversification", and "internationalization" stages, and since 2005 has embarked on the fourth stage: "Global Branding". Haier has enjoyed a growing international reputation over the past 24 years. 19 of the company's products, including refrigerators, air conditioners, washing machines, televisions, water heaters, personal computers, mobile phones, and kitchen appliances have been rated as "Top Brands" in China.

B **Chinese Passage Retelling**

Directions：*This part is to test your short-term memory and note-taking skills. You are required to repeat what you have heard from the recording. You may take notes while you're listening. This passage will be played only once.*

如何塑造你的企业形象

（1）科学的企业理念是塑造良好企业形象的灵魂。

当前，企业理念已成为知名企业最深入人心的概念，已在悄悄地引起一场企业经营管理观念的革命。在这种情况下，许多企业都制定了本企业的口号，反映企业的理念，显示企业的目标、使命、经营观念和行动准则，并通过口号激励全体员工树立企业的良好形象。"口号"通常是企业理念的表现形式。海尔集团的"日事日毕、日清日高"和"有缺陷的产品就是废品"、三洋制冷有限公司的"创造无止境的改善"等，都说明精神理念在企业中的重要性。

（2）优美的环境形象是塑造良好企业形象的外在表现。

企业环境代表着企业领导和企业职工的文化素质，标志着现代企业的经营管理水平，影响着企业的社会形象。

第一，企业环境是企业文化最基本的反映。如果说企业是职工赖以劳动和生活的地方，那么就要有一个适合职工劳动和生活的保障设施，使职工能够合理地、安全地、文明地进行劳动和生活。

第二，建设优美的企业环境，营造富有情意的工作氛围是塑造企业形象的重要组成部分。企业的厂区、生活区、办公设施、生产车间、产品、现场管理、生产服务等都是企业形象的窗口。

3 **Numerals 数字听译练习**

A 单纯数字听译练习

0. 01	0. 45	1. 07	5. 0016	4. 032	9. 83	10. 9
20. 36	42. 75	50. 03	99. 75	78. 25	66. 13	82. 25
33. 333	46. 757	71. 006	56. 777	66. 666	85. 555	

B 带有数字的句子听译练习

1. 去年这个公司汽车的销量增长了近 1.5 倍。

2. 1978 年至 2007 年，中国人均生产总值增长了 43.4 倍。

3. 中国的钢产量，1949 年为 15.8 万吨，1978 年为 3 178 万吨，1989 年为 6 124 万吨，

1997 年为 2. 07 亿吨，2007 年为 4. 89 亿吨。

4. 中国内地现有 2 亿 7 690 万个家庭，平均每户有 3. 96 人。

5. 20 世纪 70 年代，每公顷土地平均供养 2. 6 人。

4 Idioms Interpreting 习语口译练习

Ⓐ **From English to Chinese**

1. A rat crossing the street is chased by all.
2. After praising the wine they sell us vinegar.
3. a big fish in a small pond
4. Every potter praises his own pot.
5. Everything comes to him who waits.
6. The morning sun never lasts a day.
7. The pen is mightier than the sword.
8. The greatest talkers are always the least doers.
9. The greatest pleasure of life is love.
10. The government of the people，by the people，and for the people shall not perish from the earth.

Ⓑ **From Chinese to English**

1. 船到桥头自然直。
2. 无中生有。
3. 纸包不住火。
4. 人笨怨刀钝。
5. 以人为本。
6. 老当益壮。
7. 先下手为强。
8. 心想事成。
9. 虚心使人进步，骄傲使人落后。
10. 知己知彼，百战不殆。

5 Linear Interpreting for Sentences 句子顺译练习

Ⓐ **From English to Chinese**

1. Every company continuously conveys messages to its surroundings even if they do not communicate anything at all.
2. In Hong Kong，the ISO 9000 certification has been widely adopted and extended to service industries for the sole purpose of enhancing corporate image.
3. A company's corporate identity is the group of attributes and values a company has：

its "personality", its reason of being, its spirit and soul.

4. Corporate image is not only a symbol and an important invisible asset of a corporation, but also an effective weapon for corporations to compete and win a victory.

5. The advertising language can be divided into two great main categories — the advertising language of products and the advertising language of corporate image.

B **From Chinese to English**

1. 提升企业形象是捐款的动力之一。
2. 消费者的选择有赖于公司良好的信誉。
3. 有经济学家指出，70 年代的市场竞争是商品质量的竞争，80 年代的竞争是营销与服务的竞争，90 年代的竞争是企业形象的竞争。
4. 企业整体策划是企业创建良好形象、克服危机的有效方法。
5. 不同的厂房式样创造了不同的企业形象。

6 Sight Interpreting for Passages 段落视译练习

A **From English to Chinese**

China has become far more open legally because of commitments made to the World Trade Organisation as a condition of membership. But its hunger for foreign investors has been sated. The availability of labour and land has fallen, domestic capital is abundant, the local market is now understood to be among the most attractive in the world and sentiment has become more self-satisfied. So there is less interest in providing access to foreign partners.

When Danone made its investment, Wahaha says it knew little about business and welcomed a partner. Now, alive to the opportunities, it is outraged that it must clear plans with a foreign majority owner which has its own alternative strategies in China through various other (though less important) joint ventures—and it is even more outraged that Danone wants full ownership. Danone says it believed things were going smoothly until 18 months ago, when it discovered Wahaha had started a parallel firm to market similar products. It says it hopes to resolve the dispute.

B **From Chinese to English**

2008 年是中国的奥运年，对体育界来说是个四年一次的重大国际体育赛事。对于企业界来说，也是个巨大的商机和营销平台。从以往历届奥运会的成功举办及所带来的巨大社会经济效益来看，除了举办国东道主获益外，恐怕最大的赢家是国际跨国公司和所在国的大型企业。

中国企业要与国际跨国公司同台竞技，必须审时度势，抓住机遇，结合国情，制定不同的发展战略和营销策略，借鉴国际成功经验，进行全方位立体式的市场营销和文化推广活动，使中国企业能在第 29 届奥运会的不同阶段获得更大的社会效益和经济效益，从而不断提升企业的品牌文化力，增强企业的核心竞争力。

Unit 12

Economic Development
经济发展

I. Objectives

After reading this unit, you are required to

☑ practice memory and listening translation techniques.

☑ get familiar with expressions related to economic development.

☑ present topics related to economic development in English.

II. Vocabulary Work

1.	infrastructure	n. 基础设施	16. efficiency	n. 效率, 效益
2.	slump	n. 不景气	17. inflation	n. （通货）膨胀
3.	scarcity	n. 短缺	18. liberalization	n. 自由化
4.	recession	n. 衰退	19. globalization	n. 全球化
5.	protectionism	n. 保护主义	20. dramatic	a. 急剧的, 显著的
6.	deflation	n. 通货紧缩	21. subsidy	n. 补贴
7.	monopoly	n. 垄断	22. diversity	n. 多样性
8.	benefit	n. 收益	23. appreciation/devaluation	n. 升值/贬值
9.	budget	n. 预算	24. regulate	v. 管制
10.	capital	n. 资本	25. surplus/deficit	n. （贸易）顺差/逆差
11.	consumer	n. 消费者	26. plunge	n. 暴跌, 骤降
12.	deficit	n. 赤字	27. overheating	n. 经济过热
13.	prosperity	n. 繁荣	28. bubble	n. 泡沫
14.	prospect	n. 前景, 期望	29. asset	n. 资产
15.	sustainable	a. 可持续性的	30. quotation	n. 报价, 牌价

III. Phrase Interpreting

Ⓐ From English to Chinese

1. economic depression
2. service industry
3. Gross Domestic Product（GDP）/Gross National Product（GNP）
4. the globalization trend in economic development

5. financial crisis

6. consumer price index（CPI）

7. pattern of growth

8. domestic enterprise

9. ideological line of emancipating the mind and seeking truth from facts

10. push forward the building of a new socialist countryside

B **From Chinese to English**

1. 扩大内需

2. 提高综合国力

3. 自由经济

4. 第一/第二/第三产业

5. 经济特区

6. 遏制通货膨胀

7. 跨国公司

8. 财政政策

9. 集中精力把经济建设搞上去

10. 和谐社会

 # IV. Sentence Interpreting

A **From English to Chinese**

1. To foreign financial institutions China is a market with enormous potential.

2. "The year 2008 may be the most difficult year for China's economy," Premier Wen said, "It will be harder to make decisions. Anyway, China still has good economic fundamentals with huge market potentials, especially in rural areas."

3. China is in the midst of two transitions at one time: from a command to a market economy and from a rural to an urban society.

4. In the business world, everyone is paid in two coins: cash and experience. Take the experience first; the cash will come later.

5. Internet commerce is creating a new business model that gives companies, small and large, instant global reach, and that empowers consumers with information and choices as never before.

B **From Chinese to English**

1. 很多国有企业正尽力消除债务，尽快实现盈利的目标。

2. 当前物价上涨和通货膨胀的压力是老百姓最关心的问题。

3. 中国是一个有着13亿人口的发展中国家，这就要求我们必须保证一定的经济增长速率以面对就业压力。

4. 在电信领域，中国成功地跳过了技术发展的中间阶段。

5. 为了让我们的国家富强，为了一个公平正义的社会，为了让人们幸福快乐地过上幸

福生活，为了让孩子们上好学，为了使我们的民族在世界上赢得应有的尊严，我愿意献出我的全部心血和精力。

V. Dialogue Interpreting

Directions：*Interpret the following conversation alternatively into English and Chinese.*

A：It has been 30 years since I last came to China. The last three decades have witnessed the finest period of development in modern Chinese history in terms of speed, balance and stability.

B：是的，自从改革开放以来，中国已经在经济和社会发展方面取得了显著的成绩。但是，今年，2008 年，对中国来说，可能是最困难的一年。中国经济为了保持微妙的平衡挣扎于维持健康发展和抑制通货膨胀的两难境地。

A：It's largely due to growing uncertainties both inside and outside the country. 2008 is a difficult year for the development in the world economy.

B：这对中国来说是一个大挑战。

A：Don't worry. China's economy is fundamentally sound. And the Government has adopted a tight monetary policy and prudent fiscal policy to address the excessive growth rate of investment, money supply, credit and trade surplus.

B：但是政府的经济政策只能在中长期才可发挥作用，而不是在短暂的一两个月之内。

A：To date, it has taken two or three centuries for mankind to industrialize more than sixty countries and regions with a combined population of 1.2 billion. China, a unified country with a population of 1.3 billion, will take less than a century to realize her transformation from a traditional society to an industrialized one, which is unprecedented in human history. The implications of China's industrialization are that global industrialized society will double within merely a few decades, bringing about radical changes in the whole domain of global industrialization. Therefore, it is natural that the various difficulties, contra-dictions and problems which have been experienced elsewhere or which are likely to occur in the process of industrialization will become all the more concentrated and prominent in the case of China.

B：听君一席话，胜读十年书啊。我们不应该逃避困难，而应该勇敢地承担责任把我们的经济发展向前推进。我们必须要抓住机遇加速发展以赶上时代的潮流。

VI. Text Interpreting

Ⓐ **From English to Chinese**

China's foreign exchange policy is in line with the pace of China's economic development and the daily floating band is enough to allow sufficient appreciation of the RMB. That's to say, China is not against RMB appreciation but does not want it to occur too rapidly, as this would not suit China's conditions.

Some economists say that the appreciation of the RMB is a double-edged sword, as it will make Chinese exports more expensive and therefore reduce export volume. Some export-driven small and medium companies may not be able to survive and have to lay off employees. Further more, the higher value of RMB will further push up soaring Chinese housing prices. And this will in turn cause runaway inflation which could damage the economy and create an economic "bubble" like Japan.

In May, 2008, RMB's exchange rate against the dollar reaches a new high since the exchange rate regime. RMB value seems to rise at a faster speed than before and this has brought significant changes to China's employment and China's foreign currency exchange system.

B **From Chinese to English**

中国加入了 1 000 多个国际组织，其贸易国排名已从第 22 位上升至第 11 位，并被认为 2020 年将成为仅次于美国的第二大贸易国。中国的市场改革推动了长达 20 多年的前所未有的经济增长，贫困人口从 2 亿 5 000 万降至 5 800 万。城市人均收入仅在过去的十年中就已上升了 550%。由于中国经济开放，中国人民享有更多的流动自由、更大的择业范围、更好的学校和居住条件。今天，大多数中国人享有比中国近代历史上任何一个时期都要高的生活水平。

VII. Enhancement Practice

1 Shadow-speaking in English 英语影子练习

Directions: *Listen to the MP3 and reiterate what you have heard simultaneously.*

Traditional Toys Set for Christmas Boom in Europe

Six-year-old Lucas has a "Power Rangers" video game, a few robots and lots of teddy bears. But the toy he likes best is a wooden train set made by Brio, a 123-year-old manufacturer based in Sweden.

"I like to see the train go round and round the tracks that I have made. You can't transform robots into anything else. But with the train it's different every time," says Lucas, who lives in Denmark.

As a result, manufacturers and retailers of old-fashioned train sets and dollhouses are rubbing their hands in anticipation ahead of Christmas.

"We are very optimistic," says Graziano Grazini, the managing director of Citta del Sole (Sun City), an Italian franchise that specializes in traditional, environmentally friendly toys.

China still makes an estimated 80 percent of the world's toys, and its share of the global market is not expected to drop significantly.

In the end, experts say that the world market is large enough to accommodate both the increasingly popular flashy electronic toys made in China and traditional wooden toys from Europe.

Just as in that famous 1995 film, *Toy Story*, Woody and Buzz Lightyear can remain the best of friends.

▶ 2 Memory & Note-taking 记忆、笔记练习

Ⓐ **English Passage Retelling**

Directions: *This part is to test your short-term memory and note-taking skills. You are required to repeat what you have heard from the recording. You may take notes while you're listening. This passage will be played only once.*

Olympic and the City's Growth

The preparatory work for the 2008 Olympic Games has served as a driving force for Beijing's social-economic development, which also provides good conditions for the Olympics, said Lu Yingchuan, vice-director of the Municipal Commission of Development and Reform.

At a press conference on Wednesday, he gave plenty of facts on the city's growth in the 2002 – 2006 period, which coincided with the preparations for the forthcoming Olympics.

The capital city's gross domestic product (GDP) grew at an annual rate of 12. 1 percent, 1. 3 percent up compared with the 1997 – 2001 period, and its per capita income surged to 6, 210 US dollars, 1. 9 times the 2001 level, and two years ahead of the government's goal. This development was achieved through a new growth pattern featured by lower resource consumption and waste emissions, Lu said.

The share of service industries, including financing, information, cultural creation, scientific and technological research and development reached 47 percent of the city's GDP for the period and the increase in consumer spending and investment were remarkable features of the demand. From 2002 to 2006 Beijing spent 283. 8 billion yuan (about 36. 8 billion US dollars) in infrastructure, including 110 billion yuan (about 15. 5 billion US dollars) in transportation, four times the sum of the previous five years.

The "Green Olympic" concept helped the city to improve its environment and make it more beautiful, according to Lu.

B Chinese Passage Retelling

Directions: *This part is to test your short-term memory and note-taking skills. You are required to repeat what you have heard from the recording. You may take notes while you're listening. This passage will be played only once.*

农民最关注的是"三件事"

农民对"十一五"规划和中央经济工作会议提出的"建设社会主义新农村是我国现代化进程中的重大历史任务,要按照生产发展、生活宽裕、乡风文明、村容整洁、管理民主的要求,扎实稳步地加以推进"的奋斗目标充满了信心。据调查了解,农民最关注的是"三件事"。

一是渴望"吃饱"稳农兴农惠农政策"定心丸"。常常听到农民有这样的反映:上边制定的各项政策好是好,就怕下边落实变调儿、走样儿、另搞一套;个别地方还有"贪污政策"、"封锁精神"的做法。

二是希望"三下乡"常来常往、常下常新。农民欢迎"三下乡"。但他们不喜欢逢年遇节兴师动众"一阵风儿",更不希望"下乡只是点个卯,绕上一圈儿拜拜了,何时再来没准儿了"的那种"蜻蜓点水"式的"三下乡"。

三是迫切要求加快农村合作医疗改革步伐。五中全会提出,要认真研究并逐步解决群众看病难看病贵的问题,建立新型农村合作医疗制度。这是农民最关心的实际问题。农民希望尽快建立国家、集体和个人三方按比例投资、以国家和集体为主的"三位一体"的农村新型合作医疗服务体制和管理机制,实现一般病就医"不出村"。

3 Numerals 数字听译练习

A 单纯数字听译练习

0.5%	1%	7.65%	13%	48%	52%	89%	97.6%	100%
0.9‰	1‰	5‰	15‰	38.5‰	49‰	80.7‰		
1/2	1/3	1/4	1/10	3/4	7/9	1/10,000	1-2/5	5-1/2

B 带有数字的句子听译练习

1. 由于旱灾,去年的收成减少了四成。
2. 该公司的员工裁减了近三分之一,开支减少了四分之一。
3. 兴盛公司刚刚把他们的鞋价提高了 20%。
4. 2007 年,中国外贸出口达 12 180 亿美元,比上年增长 25.7%。

5. 2008 年上半年籽棉均价上涨近 1/4。

4 Idioms Interpreting 习语口译练习

Ⓐ From English to Chinese

1. The cleverest housewife cannot cook a meal without rice.
2. There is no smoke without fire.
3. There is no royal road to learning.
4. Misfortunes never come alone.
5. There is much to be said on both sides.
6. There is safety in numbers.
7. The voice of the people is the voice of God.
8. Those who climb high often have a fall.
9. The small courtesies sweeten life; the greater ennoble it.
10. You can lead a horse to water, but you can't make him drink.

Ⓑ From Chinese to English

1. 赔了夫人又折兵。
2. 难得糊涂。
3. 茅塞顿开。
4. 马到成功。
5. 脚踩两只船。
6. 既往不咎，不计前嫌。
7. 辞旧迎新。
8. 拆东墙补西墙。
9. 求同存异。
10. 解放思想，实事求是。

5 Linear Interpreting for Sentences 句子顺译练习

Ⓐ From English to Chinese

1. The State Bank of India (SBI) is the country's largest commercial bank controlling around 25% of the total banking business.
2. The Japanese have their electronics, the Germans their engineering. But when it comes to command of global markets, the US owns the service sector.
3. By comparison with state-owned enterprises, the scale of self-employed enterprises is too small.
4. Shanghai plays an important role in the nation's social and economic development. With only 1% of the nation's population and 0.06% of the nation's total area, Shanghai contributes 1/8 of national revenues.

5. This year, the Chinese people solemnly marked the 30th anniversary of China's reform and opening up.

B From Chinese to English

1. 全球化不再是一个模糊的商业术语，而是显然已经成为一种事实。
2. 我们意识到我们的工业企业是由大垄断集团控制的。
3. 在新世纪来临之际，中国处于十字路口。
4. 中国十分关注建设一个和平、繁荣、稳定的世界。
5. 中国有句古代谚语是这么说的："不怕慢，只怕站。"

6 Sight Interpreting for Passages 段落视译练习

A From English to Chinese

Ladies and gentlemen, comrades and friends:

The New Year's bell is about to ring, and 2009 is soon to begin. At this beautiful moment of bidding farewell to the old and ushering in the new, via China Radio International, China National Radio and China Central Television, I'm delighted to extend New Year wishes to Chinese of all ethnic groups, to compatriots in Hong Kong, Macao and Taiwan, to overseas Chinese and to friends all over the world!

The year of 2008 has been a very unusual and uncommon one for the Chinese people. Chinese people of all ethnic groups united in one heart and one mind, with perseverance, successfully dealt with the disasters brought out by the winter storm in southern China and the Wenchuan earthquake in Sichuan Province. We successfully held Beijing Olympic Games and Paralympics. We successfully launched the manned spaceship Shenzhou VII. We successfully held the 7th Asia-Europe Meeting. The economic strength and the overall national strength have been further strengthened. The living standard of the Chinese people has been further improved. The Chinese people conduct friendly exchanges and pragmatic cooperation with the rest of the world, meet grave challenges, including the international financial crisis in a joint manner, make new contribution in terms of safeguarding world peace and promoting common development.

This year, the Chinese people solemnly marked the 30th anniversary of China's reform and opening up. While summing up the experience, China has mapped out new plans to further reform and open up. The Chinese people of all ethnic groups are, with full spirits, pushing forward the process of building a moderately prosperous society in an all-round way and working hard to create an even better life.

On behalf of the Chinese government and the Chinese people, I would like to express our heartfelt gratitude to people from all around the world for their support and assistance.

B **From Chinese to English**

随着全球经济衰退的影响逐渐显现，西方国家从银行职员到工厂工人，都面临着丢饭碗的风险；而对于东方"同仁"们来说，可能只是减薪而已。

人力资源专家将这种差别归因为文化差异。在经济困难时期，亚洲公司会更努力地保留职位，这不仅可以减少失业，还能帮助该地区经济在出口放缓的情况下保持平稳。

东亚企业的这种作风可能有助于其迅速从经济衰退中复苏，因为这些企业无须再重新招聘和培训新员工。因此，一些专家预测，西方企业将来或许也会借鉴东方企业的这种灵活模式。

专家指出，虽然东西方企业在对待员工方面存在显著差别，但随着越来越多的企业更加国际化，以及竞争压力迫使企业采取国外的先进做法，这种差异将逐渐缩小。

Unit *13*

Environmental Protection
环境保护

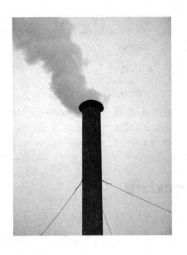

I. Objectives

After reading this unit, you are required to

☑ practice memory and sight interpreting techniques.

☑ get familiar with expressions related to environmental protection.

☑ present environmental issues in English.

II. Vocabulary Work

1. atmosphere *n.* 大气	19. vegetation *n.* 植被
2. oxygen *n.* 氧气	20. chimney *n.* 烟囱
3. evaporation *n.* 蒸发作用	21. wildlife *n.* 野生生物
4. rainfall *n.* 降雨	22. ecological *a.* 生态的
5. microorganism *n.* 微生物	23. cloning *n.* 无性繁殖
6. smog *n.* 烟雾	24. tide *n.* 潮, 潮汐
7. climate *n.* 气候	25. oxide *n.* 氧化物
8. drought *n.* 干旱	26. cycle *n.* 循环
9. humidity *n.* 湿度	27. overcrowding *n.* 过度拥挤
10. biosphere *n.* 生物圈	28. irrigation *n.* 灌溉
11. volcano *n.* 火山	29. species *n.* 物种
12. soil *n.* 土壤	30. pollutant *n.* 污染物
13. desertification *n.* 沙漠化	31. sewage *n.* 污水
14. afforestation *n.* 植树造林	32. trash *n.* 废物, 垃圾
15. greenbelt *n.* 绿化带	33. waste *n.* 废物
16. reafforestation *n.* 再造林	34. cyclone *n.* 旋风
17. conservation *n.* 保护	35. storm *n.* 暴风雨
18. dump *v./n.* 倾倒, 垃圾堆	36. litter *n.* 丢弃物, 废气物

III. Phrase Interpreting

Ⓐ From English to Chinese

1. World Environment Day   2. environment-friendly region

3. organic pollutants

4. refuse landfill

5. water and soil erosion

6. environment-friendly agriculture/eco-agriculture

7. forest coverage

8. wind breaks

9. nature reserve

10. carrying capacity of environment

B **From Chinese to English**

1. 国家保护区

2. 工业排放物

3. 交通噪声

4. 石油泄漏

5. 一次性塑料袋

6. 全民环保意识

7. 水土保持

8. 绿化面积

9. 汽车尾气排放

10. 环保产品

 # IV. Sentence Interpreting

A **From English to Chinese**

1. The attention to environment issue has become a historical trend.

2. Practical measures need to be taken to improve the environment.

3. All factories must meet discharge standards by the end of 2000.

4. By 2010, our country expects to curb environmental deterioration in the cities and villages.

5. To avoid ruining the environment in the west, strict supervision of economic development and construction in the western areas is necessary.

B **From Chinese to English**

1. 20 世纪 70 年代以来，随着中国人口的增长、经济的发展和人民消费水平的不断提高，使本来就已经短缺的资源和脆弱的环境面临着越来越大的压力。

2. 中国已修改了有关水、空气及固体垃圾污染的有关法律，为取得持续发展打下了基础。

3. 为了促进经济、社会与环境的协调发展，中国在 20 世纪 80 年代实施了一系列保护环境的方针、政策、法律和措施。

4. 进入 20 世纪 90 年代，国际社会与世界各国在探索解决环境与发展问题的道路上迈出了重要的一步。

5. 全国所有的工业污染源都必须达到国家或地方规定的污染物排放标准。

V. Dialogue Interpreting

Directions: *Interpret the following conversation alternatively into English and Chinese.*

A: Do you know what the main feature of the Sydney Olympics is, John?

B: 我当然知道。

A: What?

B: 环保啊!

A: Do you know when IOC put forward the issue of environmental protection?

B: 抱歉,这我还真不知道。

A: Let me tell you. In 1991. At that time, Sydney put forward the slogan "environmental protection", thus, it won the bid.

B: 好记性! 噢,我知道那时北京和悉尼一起参加申奥。

A: Yeah, Sydney had five strategies: save energy, save water, reduce trash, prevent pollution, and protect the environment. They tried to host a "Green Olympics".

B: 他们可谓绞尽脑汁。

A: Yes. Even the torch and fuel are produced by using environmental protection techniques and materials.

B: 即使如此,还留下了不少遗憾。绿色和平组织称其最多是半绿色。

A: That's been quite good. It's the beginning after all. I'm sure that it will be better and better.

VI. Text Interpreting

Ⓐ **From English to Chinese**

Some people may proudly say, "we are the masters of nature." It is true that the idea of "man can conquer nature" has dominated people's mind for a long time, and it is true, man has kept acting like a master and doing whatever things he wants for thousands of years. However, as the consequence of this kind of "leadership", now the "master" seems to be confronted with problems that are far beyond his control. Facts are really very ample. The greenhouse effect leaves islands and cities along the coast, such as this oriental pearl — Shanghai, in danger of the disaster of being drowned; the holes of the ozone layer make the earth less suitable to live for some creatures including human beings; the phenomena of EL Nino and La Nina leave the land with serious flood and drought; and the diseases, caused by pollution, are increasing at an incredible speed... Seeing all these facts, can we still ignore the counterattack of nature? We are not the masters of nature. Facing all the disasters made by ourselves, we, mankind as a whole, should realize that we are just a normal member of the big family of nature. Any mistreatment towards nature will meet only with the revenge from her.

By saying so, I do not mean we should give a sudden stop to any development because that will result in a threat to the existence of human society. I mean we should treat nature equally, leaving the chance of existence and development to nature as we are obtaining the same thing, and thus we will get the situation of win-win.

B **From Chinese to English**

你可曾纳闷为什么有这么多人在污染着地球? 曾自言自语: "唉, 我真希望能为环保做点儿啥!"; 曾想过要拉地球一把却迟迟未付诸行动? 这里就有一些简单有用的小建议, 让你一圆环保梦。

关掉电脑: 让电脑整天开着所产生的二氧化碳比你一天上下班开车所制造的二氧化碳还多。

骑自行车或是拼车: 显然这样做会少制造些二氧化碳, 臭氧层自然轻松不少。

种植花木: 就算是在厨房里养些绿色植物也会吸收不少二氧化碳, 带来新鲜氧气。

回收: 你不得不正视这一现实, 但是你知道吗, 就算是重复使用一个水瓶而不是到商店里又新买一箱也会对环境大有裨益。

洗东西时关掉水龙头: 这样既节约钱又节约水, 一举两得。

拉开窗帘: 自然光线更有利健康, 同时还可节约能源。

使用充电电池: 你肯定不知道处理废电池花费有多大, 何不对自己行行好呢? 既省钱又节能。

VII. Enhancement Practice

1 Shadow-speaking in English 英语影子练习

Directions: *Listen to the MP3 and reiterate what you have heard simultaneously.*

Throughout history man has changed his physical environment in order to improve his way of life. With the tools of technology he has altered many physical features of the earth. He has transformed woodlands and prairies into farms and made lakes and reservoirs out of rivers for irrigation purposes or hydroelectric power. Man has also modified the face of the earth by draining marshes and cutting through mountains to build roads and railways.

However, man's changes to the physical environment have not always had beneficial results. Today, pollution of the air and water is an increasing danger to the health of the planet. Each day thousands of tons of gases come out of the exhausts of motor vehicles. Smoke from factories pollutes the air of industrialized areas and the surrounding areas of the countryside. The pollution of water is equally harmful. The whole ecological balance of the sea is being changed and industrial wastes have already made many rivers lifeless.

Now environmental protection is more pressing than ever before. As we know, massive destruction of environment has brought about negative effects and even poses a great threat to man's existence. Indifference to these problems will mean committing suicide. Therefore, effective measures should be taken and laws passed to conserve environment. Otherwise, man is certain to suffer from the serious consequences caused by this lack of care for his living surroundings.

2 Memory & Note-taking 记忆、笔记练习

A English Passage Retelling

Directions: *This part is to test your short-term memory and note-taking skills. You are required to repeat what you have heard from the recording. You may take notes while you're listening. This passage will be played only once.*

Environmental Protection

There are still many problems of environmental protection in recent years. One of the most serious problems is the serious pollution of air, water and soil. The polluted air does great harm to people's health. The polluted water causes diseases and death. What is more, vegetation had been greatly reduced with the rapid growth of modern cities.

To protect the environment, governments of many countries have done a lot. Legislative steps have been introduced to control air pollution, to protect the forest and sea resources and to stop any environmental pollution. Therefore, governments are playing the most important role in the environmental protection today.

In my opinion, to protect environment, the government must take even more concrete measures. First, it should let people fully realize the importance of environmental protection through education. Second, much more efforts should be made to put the population planning policy into practice, because more people means more pollution. Finally, those who destroy the environment intentionally should be severely punished. We should let them know that destroying environment means destroying mankind themselves.

B Chinese Passage Retelling

Directions：*This part is to test your short-term memory and note-taking skills. You are required to repeat what you have heard from the recording. You may take notes while you're listening. This passage will be played only once.*

北 京 承 诺

到 2007 年年底，北京市林木绿化率达到了 51.6%，山区林木绿化率达到了 70.49%，京石高速等"五河十路"两侧建成了 2.5 万公顷绿化带，城市绿化隔离地区建成了 1.26 万公顷林木绿地，三道绿色生态屏障基本建成，城市中心区绿化覆盖率达到 43%，自然保护区面积占全市国土面积的 8.18%。上述七项指标均兑现了绿色奥运的承诺。北京申奥成功以来，在"绿色奥运"理念的推动下，紧紧围绕"办绿色奥运、建生态城市"的目标，全面推进奥运绿化、城市绿化和三道绿色生态屏障建设。目前，涉及 31 个奥运比赛场馆、45 个训练场馆，以及奥运道路连接线、奥林匹克森林公园等 160 多项奥运绿化工程均已陆续竣工，绿化面积达 1 026 公顷，栽植乔木 37 万株、灌木 210 万株、地被植物 460 余公顷，树木成活率达 99% 以上。

3 Numerals 数字听译练习

A 单纯数字听译练习

606	428	517	709	865	982	345	264
8, 901	7, 134	4, 768	9, 325	6, 578	5, 992	3, 780	
24, 578	89, 034	45, 637	76, 832	59, 876	60, 842	96, 541	

B 带有数字的句子听译练习

1. 2003 年，中国国家财政收入总额首次突破万亿元，达到 11 377 亿元。
2. 去年交通事故共发生 36 000 起，今年增至 54 000 起。
3. 世界人口数量每隔 35 年就翻一番。
4. 在过去的 50 年里，农业上使用杀虫剂的数量增长了 33 倍。
5. 2004 年，中国的人均年收入比 1994 年翻了一番。

4 Idioms Interpreting 习语口译练习

A From English to Chinese

1. Talk of the devil and he comes.

2. call a spade a spade

3. Practice is the sole criterion for testing truth.

4. sugar-coated bullets

5. Anything unexpected may happen.

6. become debt-ridden

7. Achilles' heel

8. Time flies.

9. Thought is the seed of action.

10. Those who complain most are most to be complained of.

B **From Chinese to English**

1. 有情人终成眷属。　　　　　　　　2. 有钱能使鬼推磨。

3. 无源之水，无本之木。　　　　　　4. 望子成龙。

5. 光阴一去不复返。　　　　　　　　6. 纸包不住火。

7. 英雄所见略同。　　　　　　　　　8. 冤家宜解不宜结。

9. 一言既出，驷马难追。　　　　　　10. 招财进宝。

5 Linear Interpreting for Sentences 句子顺译练习

A **From English to Chinese**

1. As a developing country, China is confronted with the dual task of developing its economy and protecting its environment.

2. As a member of the international community, China has earnestly fulfilled its international obligations, taking an active part in the affairs of international environmental protection, and promoted international cooperation in environmental protection.

3. We must popularize knowledge about environmental protection among the people and raise their awareness of environmental ethics and the code of conduct.

4. We still face a great many difficulties in solving the problems of the environment and development — a grand task to perform and a long way to go.

5. China will, as it always did, cooperate with other countries of the world and strive for the protection of the environment for human survival, for the happiness and prosperity of humanity, and for the benefits of our children.

B **From Chinese to English**

1. 没有这种天然的温室效应，气温将会比现在低得多。

2. 人类活动形成温室气体，从而改变了大气的化学构成。

3. 人类活动将大量物质释放到空气中，其中有些会对人类、动物和植物造成伤害。
4. 由于大量物质放入水中而使水域受到不良影响时，就会出现水污染。
5. 环境污染是当今人类面临的最严重的问题之一。

6 Sight Interpreting for Passages 段落视译练习

Ⓐ From English to Chinese

Environmental pollution is a term that refers to all the ways by which man pollutes his surrounding. Man dirties the air with gases and smoke, poisons the water with chemicals and other substances, and damages the soil with too many fertilizers and pesticides. Man also pollutes his surroundings in various other ways. For example, people ruin natural beauty by scattering junk and litter on the land and in the water. They operate machines and motor vehicles that fill the air with disturbing noise. Nearly everyone causes pollution in some way.

Environmental pollution is one of the most serious problems facing mankind today. Badly polluted air can cause illness, and even death. Polluted water kills fish and other marine life. Pollution of soil reduces the amount of land available for growing food. Environmental pollution also brings ugliness to man's naturally beautiful world.

Ⓑ From Chinese to English

水污染使得我们用来饮用和清洗的纯净新鲜的水资源不断减少，用于游泳、垂钓的水源也在减少。水的污染源主要来自工厂、农场及排水系统。工业废物每年数以千万吨计地被倾倒于水中，这些废物包括化学原料，来自动植物的废物，以及上百种其他的废物。农场废物包括动物排泄物、化肥和杀虫剂。其中大部分物体都从田地里排出流入附近的水中。排水系统将来自每家每户，办公室和工业中的废水排到水中。

Unit 14

Science & Technology
科学技术

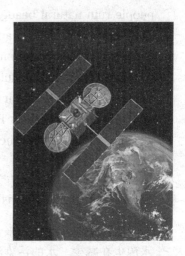

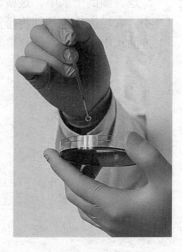

I. Objectives

After reading this unit, you are required to

☑ practice memory and linear interpreting techniques.

☑ get familiar with expressions related to science and technology.

☑ present the trend and development in science and technology in English.

II. Vocabulary Work

1. commercialization *n.* 产业化	16. academy *n.* 科学院
2. transfer *n./v.* 转让	17. patent *n.* 专利
3. trademark *n.* 商标	18. high-tech *a.* 高新技术的
4. bioengineering *n.* 生物工程	19. know-how *n.* 专有技术
5. biotechnology *n.* 生物技术	20. copyright *n.* 版权，著作权
6. bio-sensor *n.* 生物遥感器	21. royalties *n.* 版权税
7. provincial-level *a.* 省级的	22. piracy *n.* 盗版行为
8. ministerial-level *a.* 部级的	23. innovation *n.* 创新
9. cutting-edge *a.* 尖端技术的	24. netizen *n.* 网民
10. CPU *n.* 中央处理器	25. transgenic *a.* 转基因的
11. upgrading *n.* 升级	26. renovate *v.* 改造，革新
12. cloning *n.* 克隆	27. microscope *n.* 显微镜
13. hi-fi *a.* 高保真的	28. spacecraft *n.* 太空飞船
14. application-based *a.* 应用型的	29. microprocessor *n.* 微处理器
15. software *n.* 软件	30. modality *n.* 模式

III. Phrase Interpreting

Ⓐ From English to Chinese

1. cutting-edge technology
2. be capable of tackling key research topics
3. high-tech industrial zone
4. venture capital
5. cloning animals and plants
6. technological renaissance
7. technology transfer
8. high technology

9. the reform of science and technology management system
10. commercialization of research findings

B From Chinese to English

1. 改革试点
2. 信息爆炸
3. 专利产品
4. 优势科技力量
5. 研究与开发
6. 星火计划
7. 火炬计划
8. 提高科技含量
9. 实施科教兴国战略
10. 推广科研成果

 # IV. Sentence Interpreting

A From English to Chinese

1. Television is the transmission and reception of images of moving objects by radio waves.
2. Today the electronic computer is widely used in solving mathematical problems related to weather forecasting and putting satellite into orbit.
3. The force upward equals the force downward so that the balloon stays at the level.
4. The building of these giant iron and steel works will greatly accelerate the development of the iron and steel industry of our country.
5. Originally, all the matter that makes up the sun was in the form of dust and gas floating in space.

B From Chinese to English

1. 以前人们认为原子是最小的结构单位。
2. 随着可存储大量私人信息的移动产品和便携设备的兴起，如今的人连最简单的事也记不住了。
3. 现在人们已经懂得，如果食物中缺少了某些重要成分，即使其中不含任何有害物质，也会引起严重疾病。
4. 如果把海水中的盐全部提取出来平铺在陆地上，陆地的高度可以增加153米。
5. 英国研究者的一项新研究发现：想当妈妈的女性不吃早饭的话，将来更有可能生女孩。

 # V. Dialogue Interpreting

Directions：*Interpret the following conversation alternatively into English and Chinese.*

Mike： Allen. Thanks a lot for coming here to supervise us the maintenance skills of Boeing 742.

Allen： 这是我的荣幸。

Mike： Before beginning your lessons, I will give you a brief about our department. Our department is the Maintenance Department. We are on the first floor of the main building and I am head of this department. Our main task is to work with our suppliers to maintain our current aircraft. We organize all the machines, equipment and aircraft to prevent mistakes. You know that any mistake means hundreds of lives. Therefore, for avoiding any mistakes, all of the technicians in our department never work overtime.

Allen： 不要担心。我的工作就是服务所有卖出的飞机，我将协助贵公司避免错误。

Mike： Thanks for lending us a hand.

Allen： 贵部门既然不加班，员工人数一定不少。

Mike： Yes, there are 50 technicians in our team. We are re-organizing our department into three divisions. After this re-organization, these three divisions will be task-orientated.

Allen： 听起来很棒，我想知道你们的维修设备。

Mike： As you know our company is one of the biggest airline companies in Taiwan. Also, we have two well-equipped laboratories and all of the maintenance gears and equipment are advanced. Talking about "advanced", most of our equipment is automated. Automation of the maintenance procedures has greatly shortened our time. In addition, we are equipped with one molding room for developing all kinds of special gears. Of course, if you can give us more advice to design maintenance procedures for this airplane, we will be the best in the field.

Allen： 这是我的荣幸，我要开始上课了。

 VI. Text Interpreting

🅐 **From English to Chinese**

Internet use appears to cause a decline in psychological well-being, according to research at Carnegie Mellon University.

Even people who spent just a few hours a week on the Internet experienced more depression and loneliness than those who logged on less frequently, the two-year study showed. And it wasn't that people who were already feeling bad spent more time on the Internet, but that using the Net actually appeared to cause the bad feelings.

Researchers are puzzling over the results, which were completely contrary to their expectations. They expected that the Net would prove socially healthier than television, since the Net allows users to choose their information and to communicate with others.

The fact that Internet use reduces time available for family and friends may account for the drop in well-being, researchers hypothesized. Faceless, bodiless "virtual" communication may be less psychologically satisfying than actual conversation, and the relationships formed through it may be shallower. Another possibility is that exposure to the wider world via the Net makes users less satisfied with their lives.

"But it's important to remember this is not about the technology; it's about how it is used," says psychologist Christine Riley of Intel, one of the study's sponsors. "It really points to the need for considering social factors in terms of how you design applications and services for technology."

B From Chinese to English

癌症专家认为短期使用手机是安全的；但特别指出的是，对于长期使用手机，还需更多的研究结果以确定其安全与否。甘斯勒说："研究表明使用手机 10 到 15 年似乎不会增加患癌症的几率，但超过那个期限我们没有任何研究结果。"他指出，瑞典那项研究中使用的模拟手机，较今天的数字手机辐射要强。至于实验室研究，甘斯勒补充说："试管内或老鼠实验的结果跟在人体上的结果大相径庭。"但其他专家则更为谨慎一些。西雅图市华盛顿大学的生物工程学教授亨利·拉伊博士警告说："脑肿瘤发展缓慢，十几年内可能查不出来。"

VII. Enhancement Practice

1 Shadow-speaking in English 英语影子练习

Directions: *Listen to the MP3 and reiterate what you have heard simultaneously.*

There are different ways to store fish. Two ways to keep fish for future use are canning and freezing. Two other methods are drying and smoking. Today we have the first of two reports describing, step by step, how to prepare dried or smoked fish.

Begin with fish that are just out of the water. If the fish are small, leave their heads on. Cut off the heads if the fish are longer than twenty centimeters or weigh more than one hundred fifteen grams.

Now clean the freshly caught fish. Cut off the scales and cut open the stomach. Remove everything inside. Then wash the fish in clean water and rub salt into them.

Next, put the fish in a container with a solution of three hundred grams of salt and one liter of water. This will remove the blood from the meat. Keep the fish in the saltwater for about thirty minutes. After that, wash them again in clean water.

Next, put the fish in a solution that has more salt in the water. The water should be salty enough so that the fish float to the top. If the fish sink to the bottom of the container, add more salt to the water.

Cover the container with a clean piece of wood. Place a heavy stone on the wood to hold it down. Leave the fish there for about six hours.

After that, remove them from the saltwater and place them on a clean surface. Cover the fish with a clean piece of white cloth and let them dry.

We are not done yet. We will discuss the next steps in drying fish next week. We will also describe the smoking process.

2 Memory & Note-taking 记忆、笔记练习

A **English Passage Retelling**

Directions: *This part is to test your short-term memory and note-taking skills. You are required to repeat what you have heard from the recording. You may take notes while you're listening. This passage will be played only once.*

Cooking Meals with the Sun

Millions of people around the world cook their food over a smoky fire every day. It is often difficult to find wood for the fire. People who do not have wood must spend large amounts of money on cooking fuel. However, there is a much easier way to cook food using energy from the sun.

Solar cookers, or ovens, have been used for centuries. A Swiss scientist made the first solar oven in seventeen sixty-seven. Today, people are using solar cookers in many countries around the world. People use solar ovens to cook food and to heat drinking water to kill bacteria and other harmful organisms.

There are three kinds of solar ovens. The first is a box cooker. It is designed with a special wall that shines or reflects sunlight into the box. Heat gets trapped under a piece of glass or plastic covering the top of the cooker. A box oven is effective for slow cooking of large amounts of food.

The second kind of solar oven is a panel cooker. It includes several flat walls, or panels, that directly reflect the sun's light onto the food. The food is inside a separate container of plastic or glass that traps heat energy. People can build panel cookers quickly and with very few supplies. They do not cost much. In Kenya, for example, panel cookers are being manufactured for just two dollars.

B Chinese Passage Retelling

Directions：*This part is to test your short-term memory and note-taking skills. You are required to repeat what you have heard from the recording. You may take notes while you're listening. This passage will be played only once.*

汽车太阳能天窗——环保节能新科技

汽车天窗的玻璃下方设置有太阳能电池，太阳能电池与设置的控制单元输入端相连接，输入端连接车辆空调系统的温度传感器，同时输入端还与蓄电池和点火器相连接。玻璃下方的太阳能电池吸收太阳能，经汽车天窗控制单元可以对蓄电池进行充电，保证蓄电池的电能充足，同时延长蓄电池的使用寿命。而太阳能天窗带给消费者的最直接好处是，在夏天高温天气里，汽车在烈日下停车熄火，完全没有能源供给时，能自动调节车内温度。利用内置在天窗内部的太阳能集电板依靠阳光所产生的电力，经过控制系统来驱动鼓风机，将车厢外的冷空气导入车内，驱除车内热气，达到降温的目的。当驾驶者及乘员再打开车门及坐在座位上，不会感觉热浪袭人、闷热难耐，汽车的空调系统可以在最短时间内将车内温度降至舒适的程度。同时，可以改善车内的空气状况，冬天也可以减少车内前挡风玻璃的结霜。根据资料显示，与没有通风降温的车型相比，安装了太阳能天窗的汽车驾驶室内的温度最高降低20℃。利用太阳能供电，节能降温，十分有效地减少了汽车内由热所产生的"孤岛"效应。

3 Numerals 数字听译练习

A 单纯数字听译练习

965	457	349	604	872	548	781	247
9,741	8,063	5,428	6,079	4,237	5,036	7,603	
56,788	74,325	89,036	63,427	79,062	23,457	48,092	

B 带有数字的句子听译练习

1. 去年我国的平均房价增长了 14.4%。
2. 今年的小麦产量是 4 148 万吨，是去年的两倍。
3. 中国准备在 15 年内把核发电量从 16 兆千瓦增至 40 兆千瓦。
4. 我校的外国留学生总计 5 300 人。
5. 2002 年中国的高等院校总数达 1 075 所。

4 Idioms Interpreting 习语口译练习

A From English to Chinese

1. A slow sparrow should make an early start.
2. white night
3. spare no effort; go all out
4. No discord, no concord.
5. rob Peter to pay Paul
6. To be virtuous is to do good.
7. convert defeat into victory
8. To err is human.
9. To know everything is to know nothing.
10. To love and to be loved is the greatest happiness of existence.

B From Chinese to English

1. 大开眼界。
2. 国泰民安。
3. 功夫不负有心人。
4. 好了伤疤忘了疼。
5. 和气生财。
6. 活到老，学到老。
7. 真爱永不老。
8. 金无足赤，人无完人。
9. 金玉满堂。
10. 脚踏实地。

5 Linear Interpreting for Sentences 句子顺译练习

A From English to Chinese

1. It has been a hot topic discussed heatedly for the time being that how indeed the media influence the teens.
2. Software has been developed that allows computers with different platforms to coexist and exchange data on the same LAN.
3. Possessing a car gives a much greater degree of mobility, enabling the driver to move around freely, so the car owner is no longer forced to rely on public transport to get about.
4. If it could be made as complex as a human brain, the computer could be the equivalent of a human brain and do whatever a human brain can do.
5. Even if you're new to the Net, you've probably heard about multimedia on-line —

listening to audio, watching animations and videos, even playing in three-dimensional space.

B **From Chinese to English**

1. 我们正进入一个知识经济的时代，这个时代的本质特征是科学技术在经济增长中起着核心作用。
2. 换言之，我们一旦突破了某个极点，计算机将盛行起来，并导致"复杂性爆炸"。
3. 建立和运用一个城市技术创新体系是促进城市区域经济可持续发展的一块基石。
4. 人工智能的传统目标是创造出像人一样的机器来。
5. 随着计算机的发展，因特网进入人们的日常生活，因此网上聊天作为一种新的交流方式越来越受欢迎。

6 Sight Interpreting for Passages 段落视译练习

A **From English to Chinese**

The difference between a brain and a computer can be expressed in a single word: complexity. Even the most complicated computer man has yet built can't compare in intricacy with the brain. Computer switches and combines number in the thousands rather than in the billions. What's more, the computer switch is just an on-off device, whereas the brain cell is itself possessed of a tremendously complex inner structure.

Can a computer think? That depends on what you mean by "think". If solving a mathematical problem is "thinking", then a computer can "think" and do so much faster than a man. Of course, most mathematical problems can be solved quite mechanically by repeating certain straightforward processes over and over again. Even the simple computers of today can be geared for that.

Surely, though, if a computer can be made complex enough, it can be as creative as we are. If it could be made as complex as a human brain, it could be the equivalent of a human brain and do whatever a human brain can do.

But how long will it take to build a computer complex enough to duplicate the human brain? Perhaps not as long as some think. Long before we approach a computer as complex as our brain, we will perhaps build a computer that is at least complex enough to design another computer more complex than itself. This more complex computer could design one still more complex and so on and so on and so on.

In other words, once we pass a certain critical point, the computers take over and there is a "complexity explosion". In a very short time thereafter, computers may exist that not only duplicate the human brain — but far surpass it.

B **From Chinese to English**

"多媒体"到底意味着什么?

从字面上看,多媒体是指两种或两种以上媒体。如果一本书的出版者想加入当前多媒体广告的行列,那么,他就可以声称这本书已经使用了多媒体技术。因为,毕竟,它包含两种媒体、文本和图形(插图)。然而,当大多数人谈及多媒体时,他们通常是指混合了两种或两种以上连续的媒体,即媒体可以在一段规定的时间之内连续播放,并且通常伴随着与用户的交互。实际上,这两种媒体通常指音频和视频,即声音加移动的图片。

在多媒体环境中,我们可以同时拥有图形和文本,也可以增加图片、动画、高质量的音响和全动感视频,这些技术使得计算机使用起来更有趣,也更容易。例如,一个多媒体程序可以播放一段电影:一只小猫正在玩线团,发出"喵喵"的声音……这个画面可以立即剪贴到一段文字旁边。

Unit 15 Cyber Age
网络时代

I. Objectives

After reading this unit, you are required to

☑ practice memory and sight interpreting techniques.

☑ get familiar with expressions related to the cyber age.

☑ present the trend and development in the cyber age in English.

II. Vocabulary Work

1.	e-mail *n.* 电子邮件	16.	web-surfing *n.* 网上冲浪
2.	e-management *n.* 电子管理	17.	platform *n.* 平台
3.	e-currency *n.* 电子货币	18.	webpage *n.* 网页
4.	e-commerce *n.* 电子商务	19.	homepage *n.* 主页
5.	broadband *n.* 宽带	20.	download *v.* 下载
6.	backup *n.* 备份	21.	online *ad.* 在线
7.	hacker *n.* 黑客	22.	offline *ad.* 下线
8.	interface *n.* 界面	23.	informationize *v.* 信息化
9.	network *n.* 网络	24.	retrieval *n.* 检索
10.	portals *n.* 门户网站	25.	virtual *a.* 虚拟的
11.	extranet *n.* 外联网	26.	digital *a.* 数字的
12.	networking *n.* 网络化	27.	process *v.* 处理
13.	navigator *n.* 浏览器	28.	terminal *n.* 终端
14.	compatible *a.* 兼容的	29.	chip *n.* 集成芯片
15.	netizen *n.* 网民	30.	server *n.* 服务器

III. Phrase Interpreting

A **From English to Chinese**

1. palm computer
2. integrated service digital network
3. domain name system
4. Internet service provider
5. liquid crystal display（LCD）
6. information superhighway
7. cyber business
8. network administrator

9. system halted   10. punch the card

B From Chinese to English

1. 远程登录   2. 视频点播
3. 手机入网费   4. 万维网
5. 网络经济   6. 网上犯罪
7. 网上交易平台   8. 信息处理系统
9. 公告板   10. 电子商务认证

IV. Sentence Interpreting

A From English to Chinese

1. Adapting to the business models based on the Net requires some miserable changes.
2. Today's Internet is a powerful way to communicate, including e-mail, instant messaging and chatroom services.
3. As communications technologies advance and networks become more efficient, the shift to e-lancing promises to accelerate.
4. With the wide use of computers, online crimes grow and become a social problem all over the world.
5. However, just as a coin has two sides, the Internet may also do harm to us if we don't use it properly.

B From Chinese to English

1. 关注未来因特网的最佳方法是了解今日的因特网存在着什么问题。
2. 在这个信息时代，中国没有哪一个产业像网络产业发展得这么快。
3. 为了促进中国的网络产业快速而健康地发展，我们必须采取一些恰当的措施。
4. 现在已有 20 多家中国网络公司申请在香港股市上市。
5. 要想开发一个拥有 12 亿人口的市场，网络服务部门应该改进服务。

V. Dialogue Interpreting

Directions: *Interpret the following conversation alternatively into English and Chinese.*

A: What's your job?
B: 我的部分工作是在电脑上保护使用电脑的孩子。有电脑和"猫"，孩子们就可以上网，和世界各地其他电脑使用者交流。他们交换信息、游戏，甚至是带图像和声音的文件。

A： It's fun. But the danger is that you can never be sure of whom you are talking to online. This can lead to trouble.

B： 问题很严重。你不知道对方是否在扮演哪个角色，这就可能造成很大的危害。他们可能使用假名，信口开河。

A： Can you put it in detail?

B： 有些成人装成孩子在网上聊天室闲逛，企图了解孩子们的兴趣。他们通常诱骗孩子谈一些不太好的话题。最可怕的是，他们安排和孩子们见面。在性质最恶劣的一些案件中，有些孩子就被谋害了。

A： Terrible! I just can't believe it! But, I have ever heard the cases in which kids have stolen credit-card numbers and ordered things online. What happens is that, at last, the kids got arrested for stealing.

B： 上网的好处大大超过危险。只要你警惕一些，慎用电脑，就没必要恐慌。

A： I can't agree with you more. And we can enjoy ourselves online if we don't give anyone online our real name, phone number or home address, never talk to anyone by phone if we know them only online and never agree to meet someone we've met online any place offline.

B： 对! 谨慎上网才能其乐无穷!

VI. Text Interpreting

Ⓐ **From English to Chinese**

The Internet is a giant network of computers located all over the world that can communicate with each other.

The Internet is an international collection of computer networks. It was started in 1969, when the US Department of Defense established a nationwide network to connect a handful of universities and contractors. The original idea was to increase computing capacity that could be shared by users in many locations and to find out what it would take for computer networks to survive a nuclear war or other disaster by providing multiple path between users. People on the ARPNET (as this nationwide network was originally called) quickly discovered that they could exchange messages and conduct electronic "conferences" with distant colleagues for purposes that had nothing to do with the military industrial complex. If somebody else had something interesting stored on their computer, it was a simple matter to obtain a copy (assuming the owner did not protect it).

Over the years, additional networks joined which added access to more and more computers. The first international connections, to Norway and England, were added in 1973. Today thousands of networks and millions of computers are connected to the Internet. It is growing so quickly that nobody can say exactly how many users are "On the Net".

B **From Chinese to English**

中国可能成为了世界上第一个将网络成瘾视为临床障碍的国家。数以百万计的中国人上网成瘾,不能自拔,这种现象日益引起了人们的忧虑。

用户每天上网超过 6 小时,并且表现出睡眠障碍,注意力集中障碍,非常渴望上网,暴躁,或者心理或生理上的痛苦等之中的至少一种症状,即符合网瘾的定义。

那么,怎样治疗网瘾呢?

治疗方法与治疗其他成瘾疾病类似:切断病人与网络的联系,然后给予他们心理辅导,再辅之以小组互动活动,教病人和现实社会进行交流。

根据官方数字,中国拥有全球最多的互联网用户,人数达 2 亿 5 300 万人,而且随着收入水平的增加,电脑普及率提高,网民人数也在迅速增长。

VII. Enhancement Practice

1 Shadow-speaking in English 英语影子练习

Directions: *Listen to the MP3 and reiterate what you have heard simultaneously.*

When you hear the term, "computer geek," what image immediately pops into mind? Is the geek in your mind's eye a woman? Probably not.

There's a reason the stereotype of the computer geek is almost always depicted as male. Around the world, significantly more men than women work in computer science.

Sociologists understand that the underrepresentation of women in the sciences and mathematics isn't simply a matter of women stinking at these subjects or lacking interest in them. If women believe they aren't talented in science and math or that these subjects don't hold interest for them, this is in part a result of the widely circulated belief that these subjects come more naturally to men. Women are thought to be better suited to fields such as education and healthcare. Women who dare choose a career in the sciences or in math are likely to experience prejudice from their male colleagues, as well as from the community at large.

Sociologists found it curious though that the degree to which women are underrepresented in computer science varies largely from one industrialized country to another. Women are much better represented in computer science in South Korea, Ireland,

and Turkey than in the Czech Republic, Germany, or Belgium, for example.

2 Memory & Note-taking 记忆、笔记练习

A English Passage Retelling

Directions: *This part is to test your short-term memory and note-taking skills. You are required to repeat what you have heard from the recording. You may take notes while you're listening. This passage will be played only once.*

Online Shopping

With the development of the Internet and the popularization of computers, shopping on the Internet has become a commonplace in our life. Here consumers can buy almost everything they need.

Shopping on the Internet has a lot of advantages, of which the most important is perhaps its convenience. People don't have to waste a lot of their energy and precious time to go from one shop to another to choose the commodities they like. This is especially desirable to the old, the sick and the busy people who cannot go to the shops in person. The goods come in all shapes, sizes and colors on the Internet. All they need to do is to sit in front of their computers and click the mouses. The commodities they order will be delivered to them promptly.

However, shopping on the Internet also has its disadvantages. The first disadvantage is that the consumers can't see the goods or try them on personally. Sometimes, the real goods may not be the same as what they have seen on the computer. The second disadvantage is that some shops on the Internet are not registered. They will never deliver anything to you after they get the money from you. Once cheated, you will find that you have nowhere to go to complain.

B Chinese Passage Retelling

Directions: *This part is to test your short-term memory and note-taking skills. You are required to repeat what you have heard from the recording. You may take notes while you're listening. This passage will be played only once.*

因特网的三个趋势

因特网有这样三个趋势。

第一，这个世界上的全部信息，古今中外，天文地理，全部数字化，并且挂到网上，供全人类共享。

几千年人类创造的文明财富：文学艺术、科学技术、名胜古迹、传世国宝，也就是

说各式各样的文化遗产，都有人正在把它们数字化，或者形成各种文字，或者形成各种图片，放到网上，供大家查询，供大家检索。

所以我说，全部信息数字化，并且被因特网一网打尽，这是第一个趋势。

第二，全世界采集各类数据资料的电子设备，正在联成一个个网络，一个个感知网络，并且也要与这个因特网连起来。

交通监测的探头，联起来，成为管理交通的网络。

采集气象数据的电子设备，联起来，成为天气预报的网络。

地理资料的传感仪表，联起来，成为地震监测的网络、矿物勘探的网络、汽车导航的网络。

土壤水文的分析仪器，联起来，成为土质分析的网络及潮汐预测、水灾预警的网络。

再把人体健康监测的仪器设备，联起来，成为社区老年人健康保护的网络。

所有这些网络联结的方法可以用导线，但更多地将采用无线电。GPS 技术，也就是全球定位系统可以准确地标出这些网络感知终端的位置。

我们可以说："全世界电子设备，连接起来！"这是第二个趋势。

第三，所有网民都到网上发布消息，发表观点。

因特网先是有 BBS，现在又有了 Blog，人人可以写，个个允许贴，没有年龄性别歧视，也看不出地域民族差别，只要不违反法律，不侵犯人权，不需要得到什么人的批准，也不管信息是什么样的媒体形式。

3　Numerals 数字听译练习

A　单纯数字听译练习

813	984	704	485	508	357	239	630
4,946	6,037	7,259	8,051	4,986	5,631	9,028	
69,420	50,392	48,031	97,812	75,941	46,309	31,042	

B　带有数字的句子听译练习

1. 中国的公共网络已覆盖365个城市，上网电脑达520万台，经常上网的人达126万人以上。
2. 上市前一年的公司税后利润必须达到6 000万元。
3. 中国第一家电子商务网站公司"8848"开张不到8个月的营业额已达到1 250万元。
4. 美国人口3亿零700万，领土962万9 091平方千米。
5. 2005年，这个村子里住着大约13 000名农民。

4　Idioms Interpreting 习语口译练习

A From English to Chinese

1. gain in both fame and wealth
2. Two dogs strive for a bone, and a third runs away with it.
3. Give a dog a bad name and hang him.
4. There is a black sheep in every flock.
5. A candle lights others and consumes itself.
6. All roads lead to Rome.
7. All that glitters is not gold.
8. A man without money is no man at all.
9. An apple a day keeps the doctor away.
10. Don't put off till tomorrow what should be done today.

B From Chinese to English

1. 瑞雪兆丰年。
2. 人之初，性本善。
3. 人逢喜事精神爽。
4. 人海战术。
5. 世上无难事，只要肯攀登。
6. 与时俱进。
7. 死而后已。
8. 岁岁平安。
9. 塞翁失马，焉知非福。
10. 世外桃源。

5　Linear Interpreting for Sentences 句子顺译练习

A From English to Chinese

1. Computers and networks handle mail dilivery, so that communicating mail users do not have to handle details of delivery, and do not have to be present at the same time or place.
2. For a decade or longer there will be no central nervous system to manage this vast signaling network.
3. The Internet creates a channel for programmers to collaborate on software development and debugging.
4. The silicon networks today look nothing like the brain.
5. Scientists are devising a version of the Internet called "InterPlanet".

B From Chinese to English

1. 今天我想谈一下网络时代给人们的作息安排带来的影响。
2. 在这个信息时代，因特网永远不会休息，永远不会睡觉。
3. 我们要在这个 24 小时的因特网时间表内，学会按照自己的生物钟来安排自己的生活。
4. 过去两年是中国网络公司的起步阶段。
5. 中国应该对国内外的因特网市场的发展情况及网络投资政策进行研究。

6 Sight Interpreting for Passages 段落视译练习

A From English to Chinese

The Internet is the largest storage of information which can provide very very large network resources. The network resources can be divided into network facilities resources and network information resources. The network facilities resources provide us the ability of remote computation and communication. The network information resources provides us all kinds of information services, such as science, education, business, history, law, art, and entertainment, etc.

The goal of your use of the Internet is exchanging messages or obtaining information. What you need to know is that you can exchange message with other computers on the Internet and use your computer as a remote terminal on distant computers. But the internal details of the link are less important, as long as it works. If you connect computers together on a network, each computer must have a unique address, which could be either a word or a number. For example, the address of Sam's computer could be Sam, or a number.

The Internet is a huge interconnected system, but it uses just a handful of methods to move data around. Until the recent explosion of public interest in the Internet, the vast majority of the computers on the Net use the Unix operating system. As a result, the standard Unix commands for certain Internet services have entered the online community's languages as both nouns and verbs to describe the services themselves. Some of the services that the Internet can provide are: mail, remote use of another computer (Telnet), file transfer (FTP), news, and live conversation.

B From Chinese to English

你在网上约会时，运气和成功未必成正比。

你能正确处理很多事，但也能犯更多的错误。如果你真心希望网上的友情升级为爱情，那么你得遵守几条守则。

网络约会禁忌 1：不准时

约好网聊或者打电话的时间后赴约，而且要准时赴约。你也必须花心思让你们的关系深入下去。反之，对方会很快失去兴趣，转移方向。

网络约会禁忌 2：期望伴侣尽善尽美

别期望找到完美的伴侣。世上无完人，人人都有缺点。关键是找到一个人，你愿意接受他的缺点。缺点是小小的怪癖也是个性，它使每个人都与众不同，自成一趣。

网络约会禁忌 3：急于求成

匆忙发展起来的恋情总是错误的。从容一些，好好了解对方，直到聊天时，你觉得舒服自如，欲罢不能。

那时，也只有到那时，你才可以亲自见网友，并把你们的关系提升到另一个层面。在坠入爱河之前，你必须先成为他（她）的知己。

Unit 16 Cultural Difference
文化差异

I. Objectives

After reading this unit, you are required to

☑ practice memory and sight interpreting techniques.

☑ get familiar with expressions related to cultural difference.

☑ compare cultural differences and similaries in English.

II. Vocabulary Work

1.	civilization	*n.* 文明	16.	peace *n.* 和平
2.	acculturation	*n.* 文化融合	17.	ethic *n.* 伦理
3.	integration	*n.* 结合，融合	18.	ideology *n.* 意识形态
4.	assimilation	*n.* 同化	19.	mutual *a.* 相互的
5.	Confucianism	*n.* 儒家思想，孔子学说	20.	confront *v.* 对抗
6.	comprehensiveness	*n.* 包容性	21.	enhance *v.* 推动
7.	diversity	*n.* 多样性	22.	exclude *n.* 排斥
8.	exchange	*v. / n.* 交流	23.	dialogue *n.* 对话
9.	conflict	*n. / v.* 冲突	24.	interact *v.* 互动
10.	misunderstanding	*n.* 误解	25.	contribute *v.* 贡献
11.	tradition	*n.* 传统	26.	friction *n.* 摩擦
12.	custom	*n.* 习俗	27.	contend *v.* 争夺
13.	mentality	*n.* 心理	28.	infiltrate *v.* 渗透
14.	harmony	*n.* 和谐	29.	complementary *a.* 互补的
15.	spirit	*n.* 精神	30.	etiquette *n.* 礼节

III. Phrase Interpreting

Ⓐ From English to Chinese

1. cultural shock
2. live in harmony
3. multicultural society
4. cultural diversity
5. cultural exchanges and integration
6. splendid civilization
7. cross-cultural communication
8. racial and ethnic heterogeneity

9. elaborate rites and ceremonies   10. informality and openness

B From Chinese to English

1. 多民族国家
2. 民族团结
3. 平等互补
4. 国家统一
5. 取长补短
6. 主流
7. 顽强的凝聚力
8. 隽永的魅力
9. 自然、文化遗产
10. 婚丧习俗

IV. Sentence Interpreting

A From English to Chinese

1. We acknowledge huge differences between different cultures, which may occasionally give rise to friction. However, it is misleading and very dangerous to magnify such friction into world political clashes and wars.

2. At this age of information, the world has shrunk as a global village. Therefore, we should understand and learn from each other, and live in harmony.

3. I think cultural exchange is by no means a process of losing one's own culture to a foreign culture, but to enrich a nation's own culture.

4. Both Japan and the United States have transplanted culture. Each nation has a "mother" society — China and Great Britain — that has influenced the daughter in countless ways.

5. Once, Americans knew China only by its history as a great and enduring civilization. Today, we see a China that is still defined by noble traditions of family, scholarship and honor.

B From Chinese to English

1. 世界是一座丰富多彩的艺术殿堂，各国人民创造的独特文化都是这座殿堂里的瑰宝。
2. 世界各个国家由于历史、文化、发展水平的不同，选择的社会制度也不同，因此他们信奉的价值观和人权观也不同。
3. 每个民族的文化都有不同于其他民族文化的礼仪规范。
4. 文化差异呼唤文化交流，它赋予人类一个色彩斑斓的世界和丰富多彩的人生。
5. 中国是一个历史悠久、文化灿烂的多民族国家。

V. Dialogue Interpreting

Directions：*Interpret the following conversation alternatively into English and Chinese.*

A： 怀特先生，您在中国已经工作了一年，与中国同事们相处如何？

B： Very well. They are very kind. I am very impressed by the obvious strong sense of dedication to work among my Chinese colleges. Working together with them, I have learned a lot and have a better idea about China and her people.

A： 在日常工作中，您发现了什么差异吗？

B： Yes. In my opinion, Chinese tend to communicate in a rather indirect manner, as opposed to the more direct manner of us Americans. In work, we emphasize efficiency, competition and originality while your management gives priority to careful planning and encourages cooperation among coworkers. Many of us are humorous and casual while some of you appear more serious and formal.

A： 我想这是因为我们强调整体的和谐高于个人的自治。您能举例说明上述不同吗？

B： I noticed that a lot of Chinese often avoid saying a clear "no" just to be polite. Sometimes my Chinese colleagues say "yes" not to express agreement, but only to show that they are listening.

A： 相反，美国式的交流方式在我们中国人看来则常常显得咄咄逼人。您认为产生这些差异的原因是什么？

B： Well, we are more direct and straightforward than most Chinese, I would say, due to our different cultural traditions, which, in turn, arise from a difference in region, race, history, environment, as well as levels of economy, science and technology.

A： 您如何评价中美两种不同文化的利与弊？

B： It is difficult to decide which is better than which, because the cultural differences existing among different nations are natural. Cultural difference blesses with a colorful world and a rich life. At the same time, cultural difference calls for cultural exchange.

A： 对待文化冲突的正确态度是什么？

B： When two cultures meet, there may be things in one culture which do not fit into the tradition of another. We don't necessarily have to agree with each other. But keep one thing in mind：the understanding of our differences and the respect for our individualities are crucial.

A： 您对于这一点有什么好的建议吗？

B： Yes, of course. My suggestion is that people of both countries should learn from each other. I will say that in recent years, the merits of the more human Oriental way of management are beginning to be recognized by an increasing number of people in the West.

VI. Text Interpreting

A From English to Chinese

In Western business culture, making an appointment is commonplace for most business dealings. When meeting someone in a Western business setting, conversation usually remains focused on business matters and business topics. Family or personal matters are not brought up, especially the first time you meet.

Basically all employees at medium to large-sized Western companies have an official, documented job description. Titles are usually indicative of rank and status. Titles are normally used to describe various positions, but are not used when addressing the person. In the West, clear description and classification of job responsibilities are instrumental in creating a strong company culture.

Most Western companies are fairly strict about employees wearing the proper business attire and presenting themselves in a professional way. In some cases, employees may be required to wear some kind of company uniform. Any employee who refuses to adhere to company policy can be disciplined. Western clients and customers are not expecting an overly friendly conversation when they make a business call. They expect some degree of professionalism.

B From Chinese to English

美国人最基本的道德价值之一是诚实。众所周知的乔治·华盛顿砍樱桃树的故事，即将此道德教导得极为清楚。小乔治在试他新斧头时砍倒了爸爸最心爱的樱桃树。当爸爸问他的时候，乔治说："我不能说谎，我用我的斧头砍了它。"乔治非但未被惩罚，反而因为诚实而被赞赏。有时候美国人仍然相信"诚实是最上策"。

另外一个为美国人所尊崇的美德为坚忍。记得龟兔赛跑这则伊索寓言吗？兔子以为可以赢得很轻松，便睡了个午觉，但是乌龟在最后终因不放弃而赢了这场比赛。另一个故事谈到一个必须爬过陡峭山头的小火车，山头是这么陡，以至于小火车很难爬上去，但是它仍不断地爬，并不停地说："我想我能做到，我能做到。"最后，火车终于爬过了山头，"我就知道我可以。"这个快乐的小火车继续往前去。

VII. Enhancement Practice

1 Shadow-speaking in English 英语影子练习

Directions：*Listen to the MP3 and reiterate what you have heard simultaneously.*

Body language diversifies in different cultures. Now, we compare the differences of body language used in expressing the emotional feelings between China and America.

Different body languages to show friendliness

You may see two men walk hand in hand or with an arm around each other's shoulder. It is a sign of friendship in China. However, Americans strongly disapprove it. The situation is regarded as homosexual in American culture.

In China, if two old friends meet somewhere after several years, they may pull or push each other, or they may pat the other's shoulder to show their close friendship. Americans seldom do this. It is rude to touch others wildly even though he is the intimate friend in American culture.

When meeting others, to show respect or friendliness, Chinese usually shake hands or nod. In America, you can see people often hug or kiss to show friendliness, which is quite embarrassing and awkward for Chinese, especially between the opposite sex. In China, kissing is only for lovers or parents to children.

Different body languages to express affection

In China, public display of affection is rare, but in America, the occasion is very common.

Hugging and kissing when greeting are common in America, but they are only used to express affection among lovers in China.

In China, one particular gesture for people to imply their love is winking their eyes to his or her lover, which however, may be only a flirtatious gesture by man.

2 Memory & Note-taking 记忆、笔记练习

A English Passage Retelling

Directions：*This part is to test your short-term memory and note-taking skills. You are required to repeat what you have heard from the recording. You may take notes* *while you're listening. This passage will be played only once.*

Gifts to Be Avoided in China

- Clocks — the pronunciation of the words "to give a clock" sounds similar to a phrase that means "sending someone to the grave".
- Avoid giving a man a green hat — the Chinese saying "wearing a green hat" means someone's wife is committing adultery.
- Gifts in sets of four — the number four is considered very unlucky, as the word is pronounced similarly to the word for death.
- Cash — can be seen as bribery.
- Knives or scissors — symbolise conflict.
- Items such as straw sandals or handkerchiefs — associated with funerals.
- Fans — the Chinese pronunciation of "fan" can also mean "to lose" and "death".
- Gifts of excessive value — make it difficult for your counterparts to reciprocate and risk causing loss of face.
- Empty boxes — they are considered packages without a gift, even if they have been carved or decorated.

B **Chinese Passage Retelling**

Directions: *This part is to test your short-term memory and note-taking skills. You are required to repeat what you have heard from the recording. You may take notes while you're listening. This passage will be played only once.*

中国南北方的10种文化差异

南矮北高：东北、华北地区的男子平均身高为 1.693 米，云、贵、川为 1.647 米。

南瘦北胖：一般说来，居住在草原、高原、高纬度、气候寒冷地区的并以麦面为主食的人，身材魁梧。而生活于热带、亚热带岛屿和滨海平原地区，从事农耕并以大米为主食的人，身材则较矮小。

南米北面、南甜北咸：我国饮食和口味的突出表现就是南米北面、南甜北咸。

南繁北齐：语言的地理差异表现为南繁北齐，即南方语言繁杂，北方语言比较划一。在南方，同一方言区内，互相听不懂。

南老北孔：南方是无为而治的老子哲学思想的主要传播地，北方的齐鲁大地则是孔子儒家学说的发源地。

南拳北腿：南拳北腿指的是武术的南北差异，南方的拳术和北方的腿功形成强烈对比。

南船北马：在交通方式上，由于自然地理环境的不同，导致了南船北马的区域差异——南方水上交通发达，北方主要靠陆上交通。

南轻北重：我国的工业布局有南轻北重的地域特征，即我国北方以重工业为主，南方则轻工业相对比较发达。

南经北政：南方经济文化活跃，多乡镇企业和外资企业。北方政治活跃，多国营商业。

3 Numerals 数字听译练习

Ⓐ 单纯数字听译练习

753	591	802	530	416	937	484	126
3, 201	7, 395	8, 694	2, 016	4, 350	5, 378	6, 321	
73, 860	53, 961	60, 842	47, 056	24, 853	83, 607	15, 326	

Ⓑ 带有数字的句子听译练习

1. 当美国咖啡消费量达到 1 亿杯时，中国只有 240 万杯的消费量。
2. 1960 年，美国家庭每月在饭店就餐的平均次数要远远高于日本和英国家庭，三者的比例依次为每月次：1.2∶0.2∶0.4。
3. 近 20 年来，耶鲁大学吸引了 4 563 名中国留学人员，同中国文化界、科技界、教育界的合作项目超过 80 个。
4. 1990 年的人口普查显示，几乎 14% 的美国人在家里不讲英语。说西班牙语的人口超过 1 700 万，是美国最大的非英语系族群。
5. 截至 2005 年，官方承认的少数民族总人口达到了 1 亿 2 333 万，占中国总人口的 9.44%。

4 Idioms Interpreting 习语口译练习

Ⓐ From English to Chinese

1. Walls have ears.
2. A rolling stone gathers no moss.
3. A new broom sweeps clean.
4. shed crocodile tears
5. fish in troubled waters
6. Short accounts make long friends.
7. First come, first served.
8. It takes three generations to make a gentleman.
9. No man is wise at all times.
10. Offense is the best defense.

Ⓑ From Chinese to English

1. 掌上明珠。
2. 火上浇油。
3. 随遇而安。
4. 自食其果。

5. 有备无患。　　　　　　　　　　6. 兵贵神速。

7. 前车之覆，后车之鉴。　　　　　8. 欲盖弥彰。

9. 同行是冤家。　　　　　　　　　10. 精诚所至，金石为开。

5　Linear Interpreting for Sentences 句子顺译练习

Ⓐ **From English to Chinese**

1. In this new century, the far corners of the world are linked more closely than ever before.

2. The civilizations of different nations are all fruits of human wisdom and have contributed to human progress; we have to recognize and respect our cultural differences, so as to prevent any possible misunderstanding.

3. We should uphold the diversity of the world, enhance dialogue and interaction between civilizations, and draw on each other's strength instead of practicing mutual exclusion.

4. I hope that such academic exchanges between us will contribute to the growth of prosperity in both our countries.

5. Cultural differences cause failure of cooperation because they provide fuel to a downward spiral of misunderstanding, mistrust of intention, conflict and a broken relationship coil by coil.

Ⓑ **From Chinese to English**

1. 东西方文化和创新的关系是多方面的。就创造性思维而言，东西方文化的影响力各有千秋。

2. 人类历史上各种文明都以各自的独特方式为人类进步做出了贡献。

3. 中美两国相隔遥远，经济水平和文化背景差异很大。

4. 我们两国具有不同的传统，然而共享这些传统对我们大家都是有益的。

5. 文化、教育和青年交流是中美两国人民增进相互了解和友谊的重要桥梁。

6　Sight Interpreting for Passages 段落视译练习

Ⓐ **From English to Chinese**

　　One of the most common dilemmas of international etiquette is what to bring as a gift when you're invited to someone's home for dinner. In France, if your first thought is a bottle of wine — think again. You risk insulting your French host by insinuating his cellar is inadequate.

Well then, how about a bouquet of flowers? That selection may show poor judgment as well. First, your host doesn't want to search for the right size vase in the midst of all his or her other duties. Second, you must remember to bring an uneven number (except that 12 is acceptable, but never the unlucky 13), avoid chrysanthemums (funeral only), red roses (which signify you are having an affair with your hostess), and yellow flowers (they imply your host is having an affair with someone else). My suggestion? Take a box of very best chocolates you can find.

B **From Chinese to English**

校长先生，女士们，先生们：

衷心感谢萨莫斯校长的盛情邀请。今天，我很高兴站在哈佛讲台上同你们面对面交流。

中美两国相隔遥远，经济水平和文化背景差异很大。要了解一个真实的、发展变化着的、充满希望的中国，就有必要了解中国的昨天、今天和明天。昨天的中国，是一个古老并创造了灿烂文明的大国。今天的中国，是一个改革开放与和平崛起的大国。明天的中国，是一个热爱和平和充满希望的大国。

加深理解是相互的。我希望美国青年把目光投向中国，也相信中国青年会进一步把目光投向美国。

青年代表着国家和世界的未来。面对新世纪中美关系的广阔前景，我希望两国青年更加紧密地携起手来！

谢谢诸位。

Unit 17 Disasters & Misfortunes
天灾人祸

I. Objectives

After reading this unit, you are required to

☑ practice linear interpreting and sight interpreting techniques.

☑ get familiar with expressions related to disasters and misfortunes.

☑ express condolence in English.

II. Vocabulary Work

1. earthquake	*n.* 地震	16. condolence	*n.* 哀悼
2. fire	*n.* 火灾	17. famine	*n.* 饥荒
3. tsunami	*n.* 海啸	18. starvation	*n.* 饥饿
4. volcano	*n.* 火山	19. calamity/disaster	*n.* 灾害
5. erupt	*v.* 喷发	20. mudflow/mudslide	*n.* 泥石流
6. lava	*n.* （火山喷发的）熔岩	21. detect	*v.* 检测
7. avalanche	*n.* 雪崩	22. survivor	*n.* 生还者
8. landside	*n.* 滑坡，土崩	23. hijack	*v.* 劫机
9. flood	*n.* 洪水	24. damage	*v.* 损害
10. hurricane	*n.* 飓风	25. destruction	*n.* 破坏
11. monsoon	*n.* 季候风	26. victim	*n.* 受害者，受灾者
12. tornado	*n.* 龙卷风	27. casualties	*n.* 人员伤亡
13. drought	*n.* 旱灾	28. suffer	*v.* 遭受，蒙受
14. cave-in	*n.* 塌方	29. debris/ruin	*n.* 废墟
15. mourn	*v.* 默哀	30. rescue	*v./n.* 救援

III. Phrase Interpreting

Ⓐ From English to Chinese

1. relief work

2. early warning system

3. hit/strike without warning

4. death toll

5. risk of disease breaking out

6. cause economic loss estimated at 10 million dollars

7. medical supplies

8. food aid

9. declare a state of emergency

10. emergency fund

B From Chinese to English

1. 经历一场自然灾害	2. 运送救援物资
3. 救灾与重建	4. 疏散城镇或地区居民
5. 救援人员	6. 争取时间抢救
7. 造成房屋倒塌	8. 使数百万人无家可归
9. 空投急救物资	10. 防止震后疾病暴发

IV. Sentence Interpreting

A From English to Chinese

1. Natural disasters stop at no national boundaries and pose a threat to all of us.

2. This is a disaster for the entire mankind. The international community has launched widespread emergency relief efforts and showed unprecedented solidarity and humanity.

3. I would like to express my deepest sympathies for the loss of life and the destruction caused by this earthquake. I also pray for the victims of this terrible natural disaster and I wish they will rise more firmly from their sadness as soon as possible.

4. At least 10 people have died and thousands have been left homeless by severe rains and floods that have inundated large portions of Ecuador.

5. A magnitude seven-point-six quake struck off the western coast of Sumatra Island. The agency says the tremor was centered about 319 kilometers west of the town of Medan. The earthquake prompted authorities to issue a tsunami warning, but no immediate reports of damages or injuries have been reported.

B From Chinese to English

1. 中国是一个有着光荣历史的国家，过去面临类似甚至更严重灾难的时候，中国人民总是坚韧不屈。

2. 请允许我代表中国政府向在印度洋海啸中的遇难者表示沉痛的哀悼，向遇难者家属表示诚挚的慰问。同时，希望所有受灾群众的生活能重新恢复正常。

3. 自从 2008 年年初以来，中国面临了一系列的天灾人祸，包括春节前夕那场 50 年不遇的雪灾。

4. 所有这些天灾人祸加在一起，所产生的一个效应就是增进了中国人民的民族自豪感。

5. 在中国半个世纪来最恶劣的严冬天气中，暴风雪连续多天阻断了交通，使数以千计的人失去电力和基本供应。中国国家主席胡锦涛和总理温家宝视察了受灾最严重的很多地区。

 V. Dialogue Interpreting

Directions: *Interpret the following conversation alternatively into English and Chinese.*

A: 今天报纸上有些什么重要新闻？

B: There are a few stories about natural disasters. There is a massive forest fire in Australia. It covers several square kilometers of land, and has destroyed many more square kilometers.

A: 这场火灾是意外还是自然造成的？有时澳大利亚和非洲的炎热天气会引发自然火灾。

B: Nobody knows at the moment, but it has been very hot there recently. The drought in Africa is causing starvation. Millions of people have migrated in search of food.

A: 国际社会正在给予什么样的援助？

B: The United Nations have sent many relief workers there with relief supplies. Several countries have sent soldiers to distribute food and medical supplies. Refugee camps have been set up across the region.

A: 有多少国家受到影响？

B: Six have been seriously affected, but the refugees are also migrating to several surrounding countries.

A: 我昨天在电视上看到伊朗又一次发生了地震。

B: Yes. There have been a few there recently. They say that this one was not a big quake. The Iranians are dealing with it on their own. They have purchased some special equipment to find people buried under rubble.

A: 报纸报道人员伤亡情况了吗？

B: So far, less than 20 people have died, but over 100 are in hospital. By the way, the newspaper also mentions that many cities in the nation are still being threatened by floods now.

A: 你认为气候变化是造成最近洪灾的罪魁祸首吗？

B: It could be. There are floods in this country almost every year, but in recent years they have been more widespread and more frequent.

A： 看起来我国的气候正在发生变化。夏季变得更炎热。在最近的三年中，夏季的气温都创下了 200 年以来的最高纪录。刮的风也比以往更猛了。

B： I think that the changing climate is a sign that we are causing too much damage to the environment.

A： 我觉得你说得对。气候会随着时间自然变化，但我认为人类的活动正在加速这一进程。我希望各国政府能团结一致，努力解决环境问题。

B： Me too. If we don't do something soon, it might be too late.

 VI. Text Interpreting

Ⓐ **From English to Chinese**

Mr. Secretary General, Mr. President, distinguished guests, ladies and gentlemen：

We meet at a time of great challenge for America and the world. At this moment, men and women along my country's Gulf Coast are recovering from one of the worst natural disasters in American history. Many have lost homes, and loved ones, and all their earthly possessions.

We have witnessed the awesome power of nature — and the greater power of human compassion. Americans have responded to their neighbors in need, and so have many of the nations represented in this chamber. To every nation, every province, and every community across the world that is standing with the American people in this hour of need, I offer the thanks of my nation.

In this young century, the far corners of the world are linked more closely than ever before — and no nation can remain isolated and indifferent to the struggles of others. When a country, or a region is filled with despair, and resentment and vulnerable to violent and aggressive ideologies, the threat passes easily across oceans and borders, and could threaten the security of any peaceful country.

Ⓑ **From Chinese to English**

主席先生：

首先请允许我代表中国政府和人民再次向去年 12 月 26 日发生在印度洋地区的强烈地震和海啸灾难的遇难者表示最沉痛的哀悼，向遇难者家属表示最诚挚的慰问。

印度洋海啸是全人类的灾难，国际社会对此做出了积极和强烈的反应，并开展了史无前例的紧急人道主义救援行动。联合国在这次国际救灾工作中发挥了重要的领导和协调作用。

"一方有难，八方支援。"中国政府愿与各国政府一道，共同努力，为帮助受灾国战胜灾害、重建家园和恢复正常的生活秩序做出我们的贡献。

谢谢主席先生。

VII. Enhancement Practice

1 Shadow-speaking in English 英语影子练习

Directions：*Listen to the MP3 and reiterate what you have heard simultaneously.*

Here are some advice for you, your family and your home to survive the various disasters, from tornadoes to tsunamis, wildfires to earthquakes and everything in between.

Never hide yourself in a mobile home, for it's the worst place to be during a tornado.

As of May 2007, 47 of 73 tornado deaths this year were mobile home fatalities. FEMA recommends that mobile home residents evacuate immediately and seek the lowest floor of a nearby building or shelter. If no buildings are available, lie flat in a ditch, covering your head with your hands. Do not seek shelter under a bridge or overpass or in a car, and watch for flying debris.

If trapped in your car during a snowstorm, the best strategy is to raise your car hood to attract attention crack the window and warm the engine.

Leaving your car during a storm can be dangerous, so only leave if you can see help. Otherwise, raise the hood to attract attention and run the car's engine for 10 minutes each hour to keep warm, making sure to clear the exhaust pipe of snow to avoid carbon monoxide poisoning. Conserve battery power by turning on the lights only when the engine is running.

During an earthquake, you shouldn't try to get outdoors.

According to FEMA, a large number of injuries occur when people try to move within buildings or get outside, so stay where you are. Get under a table or crouch in an inside corner of the building, covering your face and head with your hands. Only seek shelter in a doorway if you know it's strongly supported. Stay inside until the shaking stops and it's safe to go outside. If you're outdoors, move away from buildings, streetlights and utility wires; proceed cautiously when the earthquake is over. Expect aftershocks.

2 Memory & Note-taking 记忆、笔记练习

A English Passage Retelling

Directions：*This part is to test your short-term memory and note-taking skills. You are* *required to repeat what you have heard from the recording. You may take notes while you're listening. This passage will be played only once.*

Don't Panic: Be Prepared

Psychological Preparedness: Some helpful tips for managing emotions in times of disaster.

Step 1: Get ready/anticipate

Anticipate how you or others might be thinking, feeling or behaving if your community enters a disastrous situation — and knowing what to do. You need to remain calm so you can manage your fear and actions.

Step 2: Be mindful/identify feelings

The anticipation can make you feel anxious or worried and you might stop what you are doing because of these feelings. This is quite common, but if you watch out for these feelings, and identify them, then you will be in a good position to manage them. If you notice any sign that you might be getting anxious, like sweating or difficult breathing, then some anxiety management strategies might help.

Step 3: Have a plan/manage your response

The emergency services may have provided clear and practical disaster preparedness advice. You should check these pamphlets and newspaper supplements and work out what you need to do. Write this down and keep it handy for everyone in your home to see it.

Step 4: Practice your plan

Before any emergency occurs, practice what you will do and how you will manage your own feelings as well as the situation. Have a rehearsal just as you would for other important events.

Step 5: Monitor evacuation advice

If there is major flooding or a storm surge expected, you may need to leave your home. Prepare yourself and others for this. Have a box ready with your important papers or some special photographs just in case you need to evacuate. If you are advised to leave your home, follow the directions of the emergency services.

B Chinese Passage Retelling

Directions: *This part is to test your short-term memory and note-taking skills. You are required to repeat what you have heard from the recording. You may take notes while you're listening. This passage will be played only once.*

世界自然灾害之最

1. 造成的经济损失最大的自然灾害

1995年1月，发生在日本神户的地震造成的经济损失共达100万亿美元，这是使一个国家遭受经济损失最大的自然灾害。

2. 自然灾害最重的一年

1995 年是自然灾害造成重大损失的一年，损失高达 1 800 亿美元，大部分由日本的神户地震造成。

3. 死亡人数最多的火山喷发

1815 年 3 月，位于印度尼西亚（当时称荷属东印度群岛）松巴哇的坦博拉火山喷发，共有 9.2 万人死于火山喷发及由此引发的饥荒。

4. 致死人数最多的洪灾

1887 年 10 月，中国的黄河在花园口决堤，导致 90 万人死亡。

5．致死人数最多的龙卷风

1989 年 3 月 26 日，袭击孟加拉国沙拖瑞镇的龙卷风夺走了大约 1 300 人的生命，同时造成 5 万人无家可归。

3 Numerals 数字听译练习

A 单纯数字听译练习

538	419	604	810	893	265	753	243
6,486	2,074	5,823	1,905	4,200	7,483	9,462	
30,954	75,290	60,012	91,243	85,109	62,754	43,765	

B 带有数字的句子听译练习

1. 中国发生了地震，因灾死亡 69 197 人、失踪 18 237 人、受伤 37 万多人。

2. 汶川地震给中国造成的总体经济损失可能高达 200 亿美元。地震造成的直接经济损失，仅在四川省就可能高达 100 亿美元。

3. 中国东部沿海福建省已经转移 180 000 人次并召回 35 000 只渔船上岸，以做好迎接弱化为热带风暴"海鸥"的防汛准备。

4. 经过连续两个季度的增长，英国路面交通事故的次数于第三季度出现了下降，降幅高达 30%，从 76 400 次下降到 56 300 次。

5. 地震发生后，截至 7 月 15 日，各级政府共投入抗震救灾资金 590.59 亿元（约 86 亿美元）。

4 Idioms Interpreting 习语口译练习

A From English to Chinese

1. A stitch in time saves nine.

2. Once a thief, always a thief.

3. A fall into the pit, a gain in your wit.

4. a black sheep

5. be born with a silver spoon in one's mouth

6. A miss is as good as a mile.

7. It is the unforeseen that always happens.

8. Tomorrow never comes.

9. The wise man knows he knows nothing, the fool thinks he knows all.

10. finger on the wall

B **From Chinese to English**

1. 守口如瓶。

2. 对牛弹琴。

3. 易如反掌。

4. 一清二楚。

5. 画蛇添足。

6. 明察秋毫。

7. 过犹不及。

8. 量入为出。

9. 一个巴掌拍不响。

10. 木已成舟，无可挽回。

5 Linear Interpreting for Sentences 句子顺译练习

A **From English to Chinese**

1. In each era of history, the human spirit has been challenged by the forces of darkness and chaos. Some challenges are the acts of nature; others are the works of men.

2. In the past two months, men have attacked children with knives or other objects in or near schools at least six times, leaving more than 20 children and adults dead.

3. On April 14th, residents of China's remote Yushu County, located on the Tibetan plateau, were awoken by a magnitude 7.1 earthquake.

4. Both the pattern and characteristics of suicide in China are substantially different from the West, and there is considerable debate about the reasons for these differences. In China rural rates are double urban rates and female rates are similar to male rates.

5. I have ordered that the full resources of the federal government go to help the victims and their families, and to conduct a full-scale investigation to hunt down and to find those folks who committed this act.

B **From Chinese to English**

1. 2008 年是中国的奥运年，按说应当是喜气洋洋的一年。但是实际上，这一年里，中国面临的却是灾难和麻烦不断。

2. 2008 年 5 月 12 日 14 时 28 分 04 秒，四川汶川县发生里氏 8.0 级地震。这次地震是新中国建立以来最大的一次。

3. 只要有一线希望，我们就要尽百倍努力；只要有一个幸存者，我们就绝不会放弃。

4. 中国西北部的新疆地区最近发生的禽流感疫情目前已经得到控制。

5. 安全生产形势严峻。煤矿、交通等重特大事故频繁发生，给人民群众生命财产造成严重损失。

6 Sight Interpreting for Passages 段落视译练习

A From English to Chinese

Good evening,

Today, our fellow citizens, our way of life, our very freedom came under attack in a series of deliberate and deadly terrorist acts. The victims were in airplanes or in their offices. Thousands of lives were suddenly ended by evil, despicable acts of terror.

The search is under way for those who are behind these evil acts. I've directed the full resources for our intelligence and law enforcement communities to find those responsible and bring them to justice. We will make no distinction between the terrorists who committed these acts and those who harbor them.

I appreciate so much the members of Congress who have joined me in strongly condemning these attacks. And on behalf of the American people, I thank the many world leaders who have called to offer their condolences and assistance.

America and our friends and allies join with all those who want peace and security in the world and we stand together to win the war against terrorism.

Thank you. Good night and God bless America.

B From Chinese to English

卡默尔·德尔维斯署长先生，各位大使阁下，女士们、先生们：

首先，我愿代表中国政府和人民，对联合国发起支持中国汶川地震灾区早期恢复的呼吁表示感谢。

5 月 12 日发生的四川汶川地震是新中国成立以来破坏性最强、涉及范围最广、救灾难度最大的一次特大地震灾害。此次地震震级达 8 级，最大烈度达 11 度，余震累计发生 1.3 万多次，受灾人口达 4 600 多万。

地震发生后，中国政府立即组织救援工作。中国政府克服重重困难，在第一时间救治伤员，紧急转移安置被困群众；用最短的时间打通交通线，恢复通讯和电网，化解堰塞湖等重大次生灾害险情，并及时组织灾区人民开展生产自救工作，确保灾区社会安定，人心稳定。

中方将与联合国密切配合，使联合国的援助与中国灾后恢复重建工作紧密结合起来，发挥最大的效益。

谢谢署长先生。

Unit **18** Social Problems
社会问题

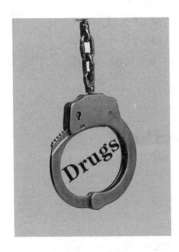

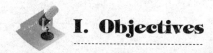

I. Objectives

After reading this unit, you are required to

☑ practice linear interpreting and listening interpreting techniques.

☑ get familiar with expressions related to social problems.

☑ deliver public speeches in English.

II. Vocabulary Work

1. overpopulation   *n.* 人口过剩
2. urbanization   *n.* 城市化
3. housing   *n.* 住房
4. gangland   *n.* 黑社会
5. destruction/degeneration   *n.* 恶化
6. crisis   *n.* 危机
7. offense/crime   *n.* 犯罪
8. transgression   *n.* 违法乱纪
9. corruption   *n.* 腐败
10. gambling   *n.* 赌博
11. poverty   *n.* 贫困
12. unemployment/layoffs   *n.* 失业
13. mistreat   *v.* 虐待
14. inflation   *n.* 通货膨胀
15. smuggle   *v.* 走私
16. prostitution   *n.* 卖淫嫖娼
17. discrimination   *n.* 歧视
18. racism   *n.* 种族主义
19. terrorism   *n.* 恐怖主义
20. anti-terrorism   *n.* 反恐怖主义
21. profiteer   *n.* 倒爷
22. bribe   *n./v.* 贿赂
23. deforestation   *n.* 采伐(破坏)林木
24. dropouts   *n.* 退学学生，失学儿童
25. protest   *v./n.* 抗议
26. demonstration   *n.* 游行示威
27. aging   *n.* 老龄化
28. job-waiting   *n.* 待业
29. guilt   *n.* 犯罪
30. deceive   *v.* 欺骗，哄骗

III. Phrase Interpreting

Ⓐ **From English to Chinese**

1. gender inequality/sexual discrimination
2. health care
3. internet fraud
4. ecological balance
5. energy shortage
6. environmental pollution
7. climate change
8. racial discrimination

9. widening gap between rich and poor   10. population control

B From Chinese to English

1. 计划生育   2. 扶贫
3. "民生"   4. 可持续发展
5. 社会主义和谐社会   6. 医患关系
7. 农民工   8. 弱势群体
9. 最低生活补助   10. 节能降耗减排

 # IV. Sentence Interpreting

A From English to Chinese

1. The UK and China share many pressing challenges such as climate change, environmental degradation and poverty.

2. The challenges we face are enormous. In 1950, there were about 2. 5 billion people on the planet. Since then, our numbers have swelled to 6 billion. More than 1 billion of those people do not have access to safe drinking water and over 2 billion lack sanitation.

3. A sharp reduction in carbon dioxide emissions is urgently needed to counter a vastly underestimated global warming problem.

4. Many of the world's poorest people cannot buy food because of soaring prices. Severe weather, shorter harvests, higher oil prices and the use of food to produce biofuel are driving food costs out of the reach of the poor.

5. The two sides reaffirm their wish to strengthen exchanges on environmental issues including climate change, sustainable management of natural resources, and measures to address forest law enforcement (including illegal logging), conservation of water resources, improving air quality and pollution control, and to learn from each other on environment-related legislation, supervision and personnel training.

B From Chinese to English

1. 中国仍然是一个发展中国家，城市和农村、东部和西部存在着明显的发展差距。

2. 我们的国家毫无疑问确实有自己的一些问题和不足，像大部分的国家一样，我们为了追求平等和公平，正走在一条漫长的道路上。

3. 我们讨论的问题包括人权问题、恐怖主义、反恐怖主义、伊拉克问题和朝鲜核问题。其中，人权问题是一个非常复杂，而且越来越为国际社会所关注的一个复杂问题。

4. 局部战争和冲突时起时伏，南北差距进一步拉大，恐怖主义、跨国犯罪、环境污染、自然灾害、严重传染性疾病等全球性问题突出，维护世界和平、促进共同发展也面临着新的挑战。

5. 双方将共同努力帮助发展中国家解决贫困和其他与发展有关的问题，更好地应对全球化带来的挑战。

V. Dialogue Interpreting

Directions：*Interpret the following conversation alternatively into English and Chinese.*

A： 你所在的城市犯罪率高吗？

B： There's some, but I don't think it's a big problem. A lot of it is petty crime, burglary and car theft. There's very little major crime.

A： 我所在的城市也是如此。此外，那里还有许多吸毒者。许多犯罪行为的罪魁祸首正是那些需要毒资的吸毒者。

B： That happens in many places. In my city, there is a very good drug rehabilitation programme. The police and courts are also tough on people who commit crimes, but I don't know if that's the reason for our relatively low crime rate.

A： 一些人相信对犯罪分子采取强硬手段更合理。另一些人则倾向于宽大处理他们。

B： I think that the best way to reduce crime is to spread wealth more evenly. If most people have similar amounts of money, they will not think of stealing from others.

A： 那是有可能的，但我不确定是否会真的发生。顺便问一句，你认为哪个社会问题最需要政府的关注？

B： I think housing is a big problem. There are thousands of homeless people on the streets.

A： 你觉得应该怎样解决这个问题？

B： I have a good idea to solve it. The government could provide some money for homeless people to build their own homes.

A： 这可能耗资甚巨。

B： I think the government can afford it. Besides, there are many advantages. Homeless people would find it easier to get jobs if they had an address. They would learn some useful skills for finding jobs in the construction industry or home improvement.

A： 这个主意不错。我想教育是目前最大的问题。看起来学校在合理实施教育方面经费不足。

B： If we are to invest more money to education, we will need to raise taxes. That wouldn't be popular with voters.

A： 他们希望政府为许多东西买单，但是却不提高税收。

B： The government should show that it is using money efficiently. Sometimes you hear about how the government has wasted money on a project.

A： 是的。政府资金有限，因此必须显示出其在资金使用上是负责的。

 # VI. Text Interpreting

A From English to Chinese

My dear friends all over the world,

Today we celebrate a special New Year with a momentous number: the Year Two Thousand.

More than ever before in human history, we all share a common destiny. We can master it only if we face it together. And that, my friends, is why we have the United Nations.

Through the United Nations, we are working together to preserve peace; to outlaw weapons that kill and maim indiscriminately; to bring mass murderers and war criminals to justice.

Through the United Nations, we are working together to defeat AIDS and other epidemics; to control climate change; to make clean air and water available to everyone.

Through the United Nations, we are working together to ensure that the global market benefits all of us, freeing the poor to lift themselves out of poverty.

Through the United Nations, we are working together to make human rights a reality for everyone — to give all human beings real choices in life, and a real say in decisions that affect their lives.

In all these areas and more, the United Nations is working for you. And it can work much better with your help and your ideas.

My friends, the new millennium need not be a time of fear or anxiety. If we work together and have faith in our own abilities, it can be a time of hope and opportunity. It's up to us to make it so.

Happy New Year!

B From Chinese to English

由于制造出口产品的企业纷纷裁员，亚洲地区女性承受全球经济危机的冲击尤其严重。联合国国际劳工组织和劳工权益组织说，亚洲各国政府需要加强社会保障项目，向经济衰退中的弱势工人群体和妇女提供保障。

过去三十年来，外贸出口引领了亚洲的经济增长，数百万妇女加入了出口企业的劳动大军，为全世界生产消费品。她们的工作使家庭免于贫困，让她们更加独立，并赋予她们更多的机会。

由于全球经济衰退的到来，需求减缓迫使制衣厂、电子厂等各项制造业工厂纷纷倒闭，数以万计的妇女正在失去工作。

在中国、新加坡、马来西亚、泰国和柬埔寨等国，外贸出口在国家工业产出中占据很大的比例。外国投资的减缓及海外汇款的减少更是让这些女工的经济环境雪上加霜。

国际劳工组织警告说，亚洲和太平洋地区今年的失业人口将增加 2 500 万人以上，整个地区的失业人口因此将超过 1 亿 1 000 万人。

联合国的数据显示，亚太地区就业人口占全球就业人口的三分之二，其中绝大部分来自中国、印度、印度尼西亚、俄罗斯、孟加拉国、日本和巴基斯坦。

VII. Enhancement Practice

1 Shadow-speaking in English 英语影子练习

Directions：*Listen to the MP3 and reiterate what you have heard simultaneously.*

A survey on "2004–2005 Social Situation Analysis and Prediction" made by China Academy of Social Sciences (CASS) shows that China is ushering in what could be its best period in the development of its economy and society in the past more than 10 years. However, five social problems, including loss of farmland and a widening financial gap between rural and urban areas, are hindering the development of China. High attention needs to be paid to.

Aggravating social contradictions is due to loss of farmland.

In the process of fast industrialization and urbanization, the loss of farmland has brought a serious problem to the society. Some 40 million farmers have lost their land in the country.

Income gap further widened.

According to the sample survey on 50,000 urban residents across the country in 2004, the per capita disposable income was 13,332 yuan for the highest 10 per cent income group, or a 2.8 times higher than national average level while that in the lowest 10 per cent income group was 1,397 yuan, only equivalent to 29 per cent of the national average level. The income proportion between these two groups stood at 9.5:1, or relatively higher than 9.1:1 in 2003. The income gaps between regions, trades and industries also were on the increase.

There is a long-term difficulty in employment.

From the view of labor demand and supply, some 24 million urban people need to work. They include the newly increased laborers and the laid-off workers, and there are only 9 million new job opportunities. Therefore, the contradiction of supply over demand in labor force has become very obvious. Apart from that, there is also a new employment problem for university graduates. It is reported that a total of 740,000 university graduates cannot find jobs.

Anti-corruption drive should be in line with political system reform.

The institutions involving discipline inspection, supervision, procuratorial work and audition in China have put a lot of human and material resources into anti-corruption campaign. However, the corruptive cases have still occurred one after another. China must perfect the anti-corruption system.

Sustainable development is seriously hampered by resources, energy and environment.

The per capita resources in China are quite low. The low utilization rate with high extravagance in resources and discharge of pollutants far exceeds the capacity of environmental self-purification. The pollution of water and atmosphere in some river valleys and cities is very serious with aggravating ecological destruction and land desertification in some regions.

2　Memory & Note-taking 记忆、笔记练习

Ⓐ **English Passage Retelling**

Directions: *This part is to test your short-term memory and note-taking skills. You are required to repeat what you have heard from the recording. You may take notes while you're listening. This passage will be played only once.*

Burglar-Proof Doors and Windows

In China, many buildings are now equipped with burglar-proof doors and windows. Some people think this phenomenon is good, while others think it's bad. And the following is just what I think.

Most people install burglar-proof doors and windows for their families' safety. There are more burglars and robbers around now than before, and burglar-proof doors and windows can keep them out. So burglar-proof doors and windows are necessary and useful.

Apart from this, they have some other uses. For example, in summer, you will feel uncomfortable and unbearably hot in a house with all the doors and windows closed, but it is dangerous to leave all the doors and windows open. If you have installed burglar-proof doors and windows, things are a lot easier — just lock the burglar-proof doors and windows and open the others. Then you'll feel better, and it's safe, too.

But burglar-proof doors and windows have their disadvantages too. Some people think that burglar-proof doors and windows prevent them from getting along well with their neighbors. Some families living in such houses think they are just like prisoners

and thus feel uncomfortable. And in my opinion, the bigger problem lies in the fact that burglar-proof doors and windows prevent people from getting out quickly in times of emergency.

I can't give any other methods to prevent burglaries. Maybe installing burglar-proof doors and windows is the best way out.

B **Chinese Passage Retelling**

Directions：*This part is to test your short-term memory and note-taking skills. You are required to repeat what you have heard from the recording. You may take notes while you're listening. This passage will be played only once.*

上海市民最关心社会问题的调查报告

上海市统计局最近完成的上海第五次群众安全感抽样调查显示，市民对九大社会热点问题的关注程度与前几年相比有涨有落，排在前三位依次是就业失业、社会风气、社会治安，而对环保等社会热点的关注度有所上升。

调查显示，23.8%的被调查者最关注的社会问题是就业失业问题。

社会风气仍是市民比较关注的，有18.8%的被调查者选择它，比全国这一问题的"关注率"高出0.3个百分点。

随着本市社会治安持续保持良好稳定的势头，社会治安问题已不再是市民关注的首要问题。

市民在关注传统问题的同时，对与城市环境、自身生活品质息息相关的环境保护问题也开始关心。

据透露，市民较关注的其他问题还包括腐败问题、教育问题、工资待遇问题、住房问题、征地搬迁问题等。

3 Numerals 数字听译练习

A 单纯数字听译练习

451	720	212	533	136	809	378	690
7,230	4,312	2,605	1,858	9,034	6,982	3,810	
67,430	25,099	78,501	42,367	72,294	65,829	84,326	

B 带有数字的句子听译练习

1. 失业人数6年来首次突破300万。专家预测本月失业人数约新增4万。

2. 最近，中国警方缴获了6.27吨的毒品，逮捕了10 537名贩毒嫌疑犯。

3. 2007年，涉及网上拍卖欺诈、窃取身份等的网络欺诈共造成美国消费者2亿

3 900 万美元的损失，创历史新高，比 2006 年同类犯罪造成的损失多 4 000 万美元。

4. 从 1978 年到 2005 年，中国农村贫困人口由 2.5 亿人减少到 2 300 多万人。

5. 我们每年丧失约 1 700 万公顷的森林，相当于英国国土面积的三分之二。

4　Idioms Interpreting 习语口译练习

A From English to Chinese

1. Like father, like son.
2. One man's meat is another man's poison.
3. Once bitten, twice shy.
4. Jack of all trades
5. Knowledge is long, life is short.
6. Every profession produces its own leading authority.
7. Pride goes before a fall.
8. No news is good news.
9. Man has not a greater enemy than himself.
10. Money is the root of all evil.

B From Chinese to English

1. 滴水穿石。
2. 白纸黑字。
3. 与人同乐，其乐无穷。
4. 晴天霹雳。
5. 趁热打铁。
6. 一贫如洗。
7. 天无绝人之路。
8. 文如其人。
9. 井底之蛙。
10. 身正不怕影子斜。

5　Linear Interpreting for Sentences 句子顺译练习

A From English to Chinese

1. The advance of freedom and security is the calling of our time. It is also the mission of the United Nations.
2. We must take steps to prevent a military contest which must be disastrous to all sides.
3. A great coalition of nations has come together to fight the terrorists across the world.
4. Many nations are held back by another heavy challenge: the burden of debt,

which limits the growth of developing economies, and holds millions of people in poverty.

5. We are committed to the Millennium Development goals, which is an ambitious agenda that includes cutting poverty and hunger in half, ensuring that every boy and girl in the world has access to primary education, and halting the spread of AIDS — all by 2015.

B From Chinese to English

1. 工业、交通和住房侵占了耕地，使耕地每年减少0.5%。
2. 中国能够、也必须在实现经济繁荣的同时兼顾可持续发展和环境保护。
3. 涉及群众切身利益的不少问题还没有得到很好解决。
4. 看病难、看病贵和上学难、上学贵等问题突出，群众反应比较强烈。
5. 解决缺水问题是一个复杂的问题，需要社会各层面进行基础广泛的合作。

6 Sight Interpreting for Passages 段落视译练习

A From English to Chinese

In the past thirty years the typical family unit has undergone terrifying changes, and sadly not for the better. The statistics about marriage situation in Britain do not present a happy picture. Of all the people aged over 16 years in Britain today, 59% are married, 26% are single, 9% are widowed and 6% are divorced.

One in seven families in Britain today is one-parent family. The children are nearly always raised by the mother and the father has to apply to the court for access and visiting rights to his own children. The father often has to pay maintenance to his ex-wife to cover the cost of feeding and clothing the children. One-parent families usually suffer great financial hardship since there is only one wage earner to care for the family.

Cohabitating is popular among the younger generation of British people. They do not have the same kind of respect for marriage as their parents and grandparents have. Indeed 23% of all births in Britain are illegitimate. Illegitimacy does not carry the same social stigma today as it did thirty years ago.

Within marriage, many couples deliberately choose not to have children in favour of pursuing interesting and well-paid careers. Childless couples are not frowned upon by the rest of society.

B From Chinese to English

就像孩子无止境的要求一样，我们人类，从古到今，也一直在向自然索求以满足欲望。我们享受家具的美丽与舒适，但我们从来就不愿去想一想由于采伐树林而引起的严重的土壤侵蚀问题。我们认为冬天要取暖是理所当然的事情，却未曾意识到宝贵的自然资源就这样被烧掉。我们高兴地看到现代工业发展带来了繁荣，但很少人会对由于工业废物导致的全球空气和水质污染问题稍加考虑。我们无情的剥削已经永远地伤害了地球母亲。

站在 21 世纪的门槛上，我们不禁会想到我们的下一代。自然不仅是现在这一代人的母亲，更是未来一代人的母亲。如果我们留给他们的是一位贫瘠、毫无生气的母亲，那么我们会受到子孙们何等严厉的批评？如果我们留给他们的遗产是一个和谐的世界，他们会对我们做出何等的称赞？让我们从现在开始尊重、关爱自然。让我们立刻开展一场建立人类与自然互惠互利关系的运动。我们坚信，有了这个新的开始，我们的孩子、孩子的孩子必将生活在一个绿树青葱、空气清新、水碧天蓝的崭新世纪，一个前景更加灿烂的世界！

Appendix A　常用速记符号

意　义	符　号	意　义	符　号
大于	>	非常、十分重要	* *
小于	<	坚持	≡
小于或等于	≤	关键	!
大于或等于	≥	奇观	!
等于、意味着	=	有关	@
不等于	≠	替换为	⌣
约等于	≈	但是	‖
遗憾、悲哀	;	与……比较而言	//
高兴、荣兴	(	空洞	○
错误、否、不、否定	×	代表	△
正确、对、好、肯定	√	优秀	★
不同意	N	属于	∈
同意	Y	胜利	V
上升、增加	↑	问题、疑问	?
下降、减少	↓	和、与	&
强、好	+	结论是	=>
国家	□	强、好	+
国与国	□/□	更强、更好	++
原因	←	弱、差	–
导致、结果	→	更弱、更差	– –
对立、冲突	> <	因为	∵
波折	< <	所以	∴
进入	∩	会议、会面	⊙
接触、交往	∞	圆满、圆桌会议、团结	O
分歧	⊥		

Appendix B　常用缩略词

Abbreviations	Explanations	Abbreviations	Explanations
AD	advertisement	MEMO	memorandum
AMAP	as many（much）as possible	MGR	manager
ASAP	as soon as possible	MIN	minimum
CERT	certificate	MKT	market
COOP	cooperation	ORD	ordinary
CO.	company, corporation	PLS	please
DEPT.	department	PROD	production
EXCH	exchange	RCV	receive
EXPLN	explain	REP	representative
FLT	flight	RPT	repeat
FYR	for your reference	RSPON	responsibility
GD	good	STD	standard
GUAR	guarantee	TEL	telephone
IFMN	information	THO	though, although
IMPS	impossible	TKS	thanks
IMPT	important	TRD	trade
INDIV	individual	WL	will
I/O	instead of	WT	weight
IOU	I own you	XL	extra large
IVO	in view of	YD	yard
LAB	laboratory	YR	year

Appendix C 中西传统节日

中国主要传统节日

1. Spring Festival 春节（正月初一）
2. Lantern Festival 元宵节、灯节（正月十五）
3. Pure Brightness Festival/Ching Ming Festival 清明节（日期不定）
4. Dragon Boat Festival 龙舟节、端午节（五月初五）
5. Mid-autumn Festival 中秋节（八月十五）
6. Double Ninth Day 重阳节（九月初九）
7. New Year's Eve 除夕（十二月三十）

中国其他主要节日

1. New Year's Day 元旦（1月1日）
2. Women's Day 妇女节（3月8日）
3. Trees Planting Day 植树节（3月12日）
4. International Labour Day 国际劳动节（5月1日）
5. Youth Day 青年节（5月4日）
6. Nurses' Day 护士节（5月12日）
7. Children's Day 儿童节（6月1日）
8. Party's Day 建党节（7月1日）
9. Army's Day 建军节（8月1日）
10. Teachers' Day 教师节（9月10日）
11. National Day 国庆节（10月1日）

英美国家主要节日

1. New Year's Day 元旦（1月1日）
2. Valentine's Day/Lover's Day 情人节（2月14日）
3. All Fool's Day/April Fools' Day 愚人节（4月1日）
4. May Day/International Labour Day 国际劳动节（5月1日）
5. Independence Day 美国独立纪念日/国庆（7月4日）
6. Christmas Day 圣诞节（12月25日）
7. Childermas/Children's Day 儿童节（12月28日）
8. Mother's Day 母亲节（五月份第二个星期天）
9. Father's Day 父亲节（六月份第三个星期天）
10. Thanksgiving Day 感恩节（十一月份第四个星期四）

Appendix D 汉英常见职务和职位

中国各级党政机关干部

中共中央总书记 General Secretary, the CPC Central Committee

政治局常委 Member, Standing Committee of Political Bureau, the CPC Central Committee

政治局委员 Member, Political Bureau of the CPC Central Committee

书记处书记 Member, Secretariat of the CPC Central Committee

中央委员 Member, Central Committee

候补委员 Alternate Member

……省委/市委书记 Secretary, ... Provincial/Municipal Committee of the CPC

党组书记 Secretary, Party Leadership Group

中华人民共和国主席/副主席 President/Vice President, the People's Republic of China

全国人大委员长/副委员长 Chairman/Vice Chairman, National People's Congress

（副）秘书长 (Deputy) Secretary-General

主任委员 Chairman

（地方人大）主任 Chairman, Local People's Congress

人大代表 Deputy to the People's Congress

国务院总理 Premier, State Council

国务委员 State Councilor

（副）秘书长 (Deputy) Secretary-General

（国务院各委员会）主任 Minister in Charge of Commission for ...

（国务院各部）部长 Minister

部长助理 Assistant Minister

司长 Director

局长 Director

省长 Governor

常务副省长 Executive Vice Governor

自治区人民政府主席 Chairman, Autonomous Regional People's Government

香港特别行政区行政长官 Chief Executive, Hong Kong Special Administrative Region

（副）市长 (Vice) Mayor

区长 Chief Executive, District Government

县长 Chief Executive, County Government

乡镇长 Chief Executive, Township Government

办公厅（副）主任 (Deputy) Director-General of General Office

委员会（副）主任 (Vice) Chairman of ... Commission

办公室（副）主任 (Deputy) Director-General of ... Office

（部委办）主任 Director

署长 Administrator

处长/副处长 Division Chief/Deputy Division Chief

（副）科长/股长 (Deputy) Section Chief

主任科员 Principal Staff Member

副主任科员 Senior Staff Member

（副）巡视员 (Associate) Counsel

（副）调研员 (Associate) Consultant

科员 Staff Member

办事员 Clerk

发言人 Spokesman

顾问 Adviser

参事 Counselor

特派员 Commissioner

法院（副）院长 (Vice) President

法庭庭长 Chief Judge

审判委员会委员 Member of Judicial

Committee
审判长 Chief Judge
审判员 Judge
助理审判员 Assistant Judge
书记员 Clerk
法医 Legal Medical Expert
法警 Judicial Policeman
（副）检察长 （Deputy） Chief Prosecutor
检察委员会委员 Member of Prosecution
 Committee
检察员 Prosecutor
助理检察员 Assistant Prosecutor
监狱长 Warden
律师 Lawyer
公证员 Notary Public
总警监 Commissioner General
警监 Commissioner
警督 Supervisor
警司 Superintendent
警员 Constable

社会团体

会长 President
主席 Chairman
名誉顾问 Honorary Adviser
理事长 President
理事 Trustee/Council Member
总干事 Director-General
总监 Director

教育、科研、文化、卫生

科学院院长 President （Academies）
主席团执行主席 Executive Chairman
学部主任 Division Chairman
院士 Academician
大学校长 President/Chancellor
中学校长 Principal
小学校长 Headmaster
学院院长 Dean of College
校董事会董事 Trustee, Board of Trustees
教务主任 Dean of Studies

总务长 Dean of General Affairs
注册主管 Registrar
系主任 Department Chairman/Department Head
客座教授 Visiting Professor
交换教授 Exchange Professor
名誉教授 Honorary Professor
终身教授 Lifetime Professor
外籍教授 Foreign Professor
班主任 Class Adviser
特级教师 Teacher of Special Grade
研究所所长 Director, Research Institute
研究员 （正高） （Full） Professor
副研究员 Associate Professor
助理研究 Research Associate
研究实习员 Research Assistant
教授 （Full） Professor
副教授 Associate Professor
讲师 Lecturer
助教 Assistant
高级讲师 （副高） Senior Lecturer
讲师 Lecturer
助理讲师 （初） Assistant Lecturer
教员 Teacher
中学高级教师 （副高） Senior Teacher
中学一级教师 First-grade Teacher（Secondary
 School）
小学高级教师 （中） Senior Teacher
小学一级教师 First-grade Teacher （Primary
 School）
教授级高级工程师 （正高） Professor of
 Engineering
高级工程师 （副高） Senior Engineer
工程师 Engineer
助理工程师 Assistant Engineer
技术员 Technician
高级实验师 （高） Senior Experimentalist
实验师 （中） Experimentalist
助理实验师 Assistant Experimentalist
实验员 Laboratory Technician

研究馆员（正高）Professor of Library Science

副研究馆员 Associate Professor of Library Science

馆员 Librarian

助理馆员 Library Assistant

管理员 Clerk

研究馆员（正高）Professor of Archives Science

副研究馆员 Associate Professor of Archives Science

馆员 Archivist

助理馆员 Assistant Archivist

管理员 File Clerk

研究馆员（正高）Professor of Relics and Museology

副研究馆员 Associate Professor of Relics and Museology

馆员 Museologist

助理馆员 Assistant Museologist

文博管理员 Conservator

主任医师（正高）Professor of Treatment

副主任医师 Associate Professor of Treatment

主治医师（中）Doctor-in-charge

医师 Doctor

医士 Assistant Doctor

主任药师（正高）Professor of Pharmacy

副主任药师 Associate Professor of Pharmacy

主管药师 Pharmacist-in-charge

药师 Pharmacist

药士 Assistant Pharmacist

主任护师（正高）Professor of Nursing

副主任护师 Associate Professor of Nursing

主管护师 Nurse-in-charge

护师 Nurse Practitioner

护士 Nurse/Nurse's Aide

主任技师（正高）Full Senior Technologist

副主任技师 Associate Senior Technologist

主管技师 Technologist-in-charge

技师 Technologist

技士 Technician

高级编辑（正高）Full Senior Editor

主任编辑（副高）Associate Senior Editor

编辑 Editor

助理编辑 Assistant Editor

高级记者（正高）Full Senior Reporter

主任记者（副高）Associate Senior Reporter

记者 Reporter

助理记者 Assistant Reporter

编审（正高）Professor of Editorship/Full Senior Editor

副编审 Associate Professor of Editorship/ Associate Senior Editor

编辑（中）Editor

助理编辑（初）Assistant Editor

技术编辑（中）Technical Editor

助理技术编辑（初）Assistant Technical Editor

技术设计员（初）Technical Designer

译审（正高）Professor of Translation/Full Senior Translator

副译审 Associate Professor of Translation/ Associate Senior Translator

口译员 Interpreter

翻译 Translator

助理翻译 Assistant Translator

播音指导（正高）Director of Announcing

主任播音员（副高）Chief Announcer

工商管理

首席执行官 CEO（Chief Executive Officer）

董事长 Chairman

执行董事 Executive Director

总裁 President

执行总裁 Executive President

执行副总裁 Executive Vice President

总经理 General Manager

副总经理 Deputy General Manager

经理 Manager

副经理 Deputy Manager
助理经理 Assistant Manager
公关部经理 PR Manager
营业部经理 Business Manager
销售部经理 Sales Manager
推销员 Salesman
采购员 Purchaser
售货员 Sales Clerk
领班 Captain
经纪人 Broker
高级经济师 Senior Economist
高级会计师 Senior Accountant
注册会计师 Certified Public Accountant
出纳员 Cashier
审计师 Senior Auditor
审计员 Auditing Clerk
统计师 Statistician
统计员 Statistical Clerk
厂长 Factory Manager
车间主任 Workshop Supervisor
工段长 Section Chief
作业班长 Foreman
仓库管理员 Storekeeper
教授级高级工程师 Professor of Engineering
高级工程师 Senior Engineer
技师 Technician
建筑师 Architect
设计师 Designer
机械师 Mechanic
化验员 Chemical Analyst
质检员 Quality Inspector

人力资源

人事总监 Human Resources Director
人事经理 Human Resources Manager
人事主管 Human Resources Supervisor
人事专员 Human Resources Specialist
人事助理 Human Resources Assistant

招聘经理/主管 Recruiting Manager/Supervisor
招聘专员/助理 Recruiting Specialist/Assistant
薪资福利经理/主管 Compensation & Benefits Manager/Supervisor
薪资福利专员/助理 Compensation & Benefits Specialist/Assistant
培训经理/主管 Training Manager/Supervisor
培训专员/助理 Training Specialist/Assistant

行政、后勤

行政总监 Admin Director
行政经理/主管 Admin Manager/Supervisor
行政专员/助理 Admin Staff/Assistant
经理助理/秘书 Executive Assistant/Secretary
前台接待/总机 Receptionist
资料管理员 Information/Data Management Specialist
电脑操作员/打字员 Computer Operator/Typist

咨询、顾问

专业顾问 Senior Consultant
咨询总监 Consulting Director/Partner
咨询经理 Consulting Manager
咨询员 Consultant

服务

美容/健身顾问 Exercise Coach/Fitness Trainer
餐饮/娱乐经理 Banquet Services Manager
宾馆/酒店经理 Reception Manager
领班 Supervisor
服务员/乘务员 Service Staff/Conductor
营业员 Shop Assistant/Salesperson
厨师 Cook
导游/旅行顾问 Tour Guide/Travel Agent
司机 Chauffeur/Driver
保安 Security
接线员 Operator
寻呼员/话务员 Paging Operator

参 考 文 献

[1] 上海市外语口译岗位资格证书考试委员会，上海市高校浦东继续教育中心．上海市英语中级口译岗位资格证书考试大纲：2008 年版 [M]．上海：上海外语教育出版社，2008．

[2] 上海市外语口译岗位资格证书考试委员会，上海市高校浦东继续教育中心．上海市英语高级口译岗位资格证书考试大纲：2006 年版 [M]．上海：上海外语教育出版社，2006．

[3] 上海市外语口译岗位资格证书考试委员会，上海市高校浦东继续教育中心．上海市英语口译基础能力证书考试大纲：2005 年版 [M]．上海：上海外语教育出版社，2005．

[4] 中国外文局全国翻译专业资格（水平）考试办公室．二级口译英语同声传译类考试大纲 [M]．北京：外文出版社，2005．

[5] 罗杏焕．基础口译教程：B 级 [M]．上海：上海外语教育出版社，2006．

[6] 齐伟钧，陈汉生，华汀汀，等．新编英语听力与口译 [M]．上海：上海外语教育出版社，2008．

[7] 钟述孔．实用口译手册 [M]．北京：中国对外翻译出版公司，1999．

[8] 徐海铭．实用英汉汉英口译教程 [M]．南京：南京师范大学出版社，2004．

[9] 朱佩芬．实用英汉口译技巧 [M]．上海：华东理工大学出版社，1995．

[10] 杨辉．实用英汉口译教程 [M]．上海：复旦大学出版社，2003．

[11] 崔永禄．实用英语口译（英汉）新编 [M]．天津：南开大学出版社，1994．

[12] 李小川．实用英语口译教程 [M]．重庆：重庆大学出版社，2002．

[13] 冯建忠．实用英语口译教程 [M]．南京：译林出版社，2002．

[14] 林超伦．实战口译 [M]．北京：外语教学与研究出版社，2004．

[15] 侯国金．同声口译金话筒 [M]．大连：大连理工大学出版社，2003．

[16] 王大伟．现场汉英口译技巧与评析 [M]．上海：上海世界图书出版公司，2000．

[17] 吴冰．现代汉译英口译教程 [M]．北京：外语教学研究出版社，2004．

[18] 林郁如，雷天放．新编英语口译教程 [M]．上海：上海外语教育出版社，1999．

[19] 刘宓庆．口笔译理论研究 [M]．北京：中国对外翻译出版公司，2004．

[20] 梅德明．英语口译资格考试分类词汇精编 [M]．北京：人民教育出版社，2003．

[21] 梅德明．英语口译实务 [M]．北京：外文出版社，2004．

[22] 梅德明．中级口译教程 [M]．3 版．上海：上海外语教育出版社，2008．

[23] 李长栓．汉英口译入门 [M]．北京：外语教学与研究出版社，2000．

[24] 赛莱丝科维奇．口译技巧 [M]．孙慧双，译．北京：北京出版社，1979．

[25] 厦门大学口译教学小组．口译教程 [M]．上海：上海外语教育出版社，2006．

[26] 杨承淑．口译教学研究：理论与实践 [M]．北京：中国对外翻译出版公司，2005．

[27] 吕国军．口译与口译教学研究 [M]．北京：外语教学与研究出版社，2004．

[28] 王红卫，张立玉．商务英语英汉口译 [M]．武汉：武汉大学出版社，2004．

［29］吴钟明．英语口译笔记法实战指导［M］．武汉：武汉大学出版社，2005．

［30］仲伟合．英语口译教程：上册［M］．北京：高等教育出版社，2006．

［31］仲伟合．英汉同声传译教程［M］．北京：高等教育出版社，2007．

［32］徐小贞．商务现场口译［M］．北京：外语教学与研究出版社，2007．

［33］李天舒．最新简明英语口译教程［M］．北京：世界图书出版公司，2003．

［34］姚林生．英语口译自我操练［M］．上海：上海辞书出版社，2005．